"THE AMERICAN SCHOLAR" TODAY

EMERSON'S ESSAY AND SOME CRITICAL VIEWS

"But do your thing, and I shall know you. Do your work and you shall reinforce yourself. A man must consider what a blind-man's-buff is this game of conformity." R. W. Emerson, *Essays* (Boston: James Munroe and Company, 1841), p. 45.

"THE AMERICAN SCHOLAR" TODAY

EMERSON'S ESSAY AND SOME CRITICAL VIEWS

Edited by C. DAVID MEAD

Michigan State University

DODD, MEAD & COMPANY
New York   1970

PREFACE

For many reasons the idea of the American scholar is a rewarding one for the student to explore. Emerson's essay, which serves as a source and focus of the topic, is perhaps the most influential address ever made before an American college audience and remains a classic document in American literary and cultural history. Although critical discussion of the nature and function of the scholar and intellectual has continued since Emerson's time, it has never been as intense and widespread as it is now, especially in the universities. In the language of today's student movement, the concept of the American scholar is relevant to the shaping of the student's life and to the aims of his college or university. Emerson speaks across a century to the alienation and anonymity of the modern student, to the character and quality of his mind, and especially to the values in his evolving personal philosophy.

When Emerson delivered "The American Scholar" at Harvard College on August 31, 1837, his subject was already a familiar one in earlier Phi Beta Kappa orations, and Emerson had for at least two years given serious thought to the life of the intellectual in America. A month before making his address, he wrote in his journal:

> If the All-wise would give me light, I should write for the Cambridge men a theory of the Scholar's office. It is not all books which it behooves him to know, least of all to be a bookworshipper, but he must be able to read in all books that which alone gives value to books—in all to read one, the one incorruptible text of Truth. That alone of their style is intelligible, acceptable to him.

This journal entry aptly summarizes Emerson's intentions in the essay: to define what he means by the term "scholar" and to explain the scholar's "office" —that is, his relation to books and the world about him.

Ever since that inspired hour in 1837 when Emerson pronounced what Oliver Wendell Holmes described as "our Intellectual Declaration of Independence," writers and thinkers have returned to his address to find new

5

meanings applicable to successive generations of college students. Emerson's own contemporaries felt the striking impact of his words. In *My Study Windows* (1871), James Russell Lowell called the oration "an event without any former parallel in our literary annals, a scene to be always treasured in the memory for its picturesqueness and its inspiration." Dr. Holmes remarked in his biography, *Ralph Waldo Emerson* (1885), that the students who heard the address "went out from it as if a prophet had been proclaiming to them, 'Thus saith the Lord.'" Thomas Carlyle wrote Emerson from England: "I could have *wept* to read that speech; the clear high melody of it went tingling through my heart. . . ." Such responses to Emerson's essay did not end with his own time. The twentieth century has seen an increasing number of critical estimates of his achievement.

This book is designed to bring together in convenient form the basic materials for a study in depth of the idea of the American scholar. Emerson uses the term "scholar" as a broad designation which could variously be applied to the intellectual, the college student, the writer and thinker, the statesman, the college professor; but the main emphasis in this book is of course on the scholar as college student, or conversely, the college student as the American scholar. Included here are Emerson's original address and four critical essays which testify to the vitality of the idea of the scholar and interpret it for readers in more recent times. Bliss Perry's essay applies Emerson's view of the American scholar to the 1920's, John Erskine relates the scholar to the 1930's, Henry Nash Smith to the late 1950's and early 1960's, and Philip H. Rhinelander to the end of the 1960's. Each of the essays is followed by a series of questions to be used as a basis for oral or written discussion.

Emerson's address and the additional essays offer various views of the scholar, but still other perspectives are possible. Indeed a major purpose of this book is to stimulate the student of the 1970's to reach original, thoughtful conclusions about himself—the American scholar—and his relationship to his rapidly changing college environment and to the turbulent society of which it is a part.

The present text of "The American Scholar" is that of the standard or Centenary Edition of Emerson's writings. The original pagination of that edition is indicated in the text of Emerson's essay.

C. David Mead

CONTENTS

"THE AMERICAN SCHOLAR" TODAY

EMERSON'S ESSAY AND SOME CRITICAL VIEWS

TEXT OF
"THE AMERICAN SCHOLAR"

THE AMERICAN SCHOLAR

Mr. President and Gentlemen:

I GREET you on the recommencement of our literary year.[1] Our anniversary is one of hope, and, perhaps, not enough of labor. We do not meet for games of strength or skill, for the recitation of histories, tragedies, and odes, like the ancient Greeks; for parliaments of love and poesy, like the Troubadours; nor for the advancement of science, like our contemporaries in the British and European capitals. Thus far, our holiday has been simply a friendly sign of the survival of the love of letters amongst a people too busy to give to letters any more. As such it is precious as the sign of an indestructible instinct. Perhaps the time is already come when it ought to be, and will be, something else; when the sluggard intellect of this continent will look from under its iron lids and fill the postponed expectation of the world with something better than the exertions of mechanical skill. Our day of dependence, our long apprenticeship to the learning of other lands, draws to a close. [82] The millions that around us are rushing into life, cannot always be fed on the sere remains of foreign harvests. Events, actions arise, that must be sung, that will sing themselves. Who can doubt that poetry will revive and lead in a new age, as the star in the constellation Harp, which now flames in our zenith, astronomers announce, shall one day be the pole-star for a thousand years?

In this hope I accept the topic which not only usage but the nature of our association seem to prescribe to this day,—the American Scholar. Year by year we come up hither to read one more chapter of his biography. Let us inquire what light new days and events have thrown on his character and his hopes.

It is one of those fables which out of an unknown antiquity convey an unlooked-for wisdom, that the gods, in the beginning, divided Man into men,

[1] Addressing the presiding officer and other members of Phi Beta Kappa at the Harvard chapter's annual meeting, Emerson also used the occasion to celebrate the new academic or "literary" year, which usually began about September 1.

13

that he might be more helpful to himself; just as the hand was divided into fingers, the better to answer its end.

The old fable covers a doctrine ever new and sublime; that there is One Man,—present to all particular men only partially, or through one faculty; and that you must take the whole society to find the whole man. Man is not a farmer, [83] or a professor, or an engineer, but he is all. Man is priest, and scholar, and statesman, and producer, and soldier. In the *divided* or social state these functions are parcelled out to individuals, each of whom aims to do his stint of the joint work, whilst each other performs his. The fable implies that the individual, to possess himself, must sometimes return from his own labor to embrace all the other laborers. But, unfortunately, this original unit, this fountain of power, has been so distributed to multitudes, has been so minutely subdivided and peddled out, that it is spilled into drops, and cannot be gathered. The state of society is one in which the members have suffered amputation from the trunk, and strut about so many walking monsters, —a good finger, a neck, a stomach, an elbow, but never a man.

Man is thus metamorphosed into a thing, into many things. The planter, who is Man sent out into the field to gather food, is seldom cheered by any idea of the true dignity of his ministry. He sees his bushel and his cart, and nothing beyond, and sinks into the farmer, instead of Man on the farm. The tradesman scarcely ever gives an ideal worth to his work, but is ridden by the routine of his craft, and the soul is subject [84] to dollars. The priest becomes a form; the attorney a statute-book; the mechanic a machine; the sailor a rope of the ship.

In this distribution of functions the scholar is the delegated intellect. In the right state he is *Man Thinking*. In the degenerate state, when the victim of society, he tends to become a mere thinker, or still worse, the parrot of other men's thinking.

In this view of him, as Man Thinking, the theory of his office is contained. Him Nature solicits with all her placid, all her monitory pictures; him the past instructs; him the future invites. Is not indeed every man a student, and do not all things exist for the student's behoof? And, finally, is not the true scholar the only true master? But the old oracle said, "All things have two handles: beware of the wrong one." In life, too often, the scholar errs with mankind and forfeits his privilege. Let us see him in his school, and consider him in reference to the main influences he receives.

I. The first in time and the first in importance of the influences upon the mind is that of nature. Every day, the sun; and, after sunset, Night and her stars. Ever the winds blow; ever [85] the grass grows. Every day, men and women, conversing—beholding and beholden. The scholar is he of all men whom this spectacle most engages. He must settle its value in his mind. What is nature to him? There is never a beginning, there is never an end, to the inexplicable continuity of this web of God, but always circular power return-ing into itself. Therein it resembles his own spirit, whose beginning, whose ending, he never can find,—so entire, so boundless. Far too as her splendors shine, system on system shooting like rays, upward, downward, without centre, without circumference,—in the mass and in the particle, Nature has-tens to render account of herself to the mind. Classification begins. To the young mind every thing is individual, stands by itself. By and by, it finds how to join two things and see in them one nature; then three, then three thou-sand; and so, tyrannized over by its own unifying instinct, it goes on tying things together, diminishing anomalies, discovering roots running under ground whereby contrary and remote things cohere and flower out from one stem. It presently learns that since the dawn of history there has been a con-stant accumulation and classifying of facts. But what is classification but the perceiving that [86] these objects are not chaotic, and are not foreign, but have a law which is also a law of the human mind? The astronomer discovers that geometry, a pure abstraction of the human mind, is the measure of plane-tary motion. The chemist finds proportions and intelligible method throughout matter; and science is nothing but the finding of analogy, identity, in the most remote parts. The ambitious soul sits down before each refractory fact; one after another reduces all strange constitutions, all new powers, to their class and their law, and goes on forever to animate the last fibre of organization, the outskirts of nature, by insight.

Thus to him, to this schoolboy under the bending dome of day, is suggested that he and it proceed from one root; one is leaf and one is flower; relation, sympathy, stirring in every vein. And what is that root? Is not that the soul of his soul? A thought too bold; a dream too wild. Yet when this spiritual light shall have revealed the law of more earthly natures,—when he has learned to worship the soul, and to see that the natural philosophy that now is, is only the first gropings of its gigantic hand, he shall look forward to an ever ex-panding knowledge as to a becoming creator. He shall see [87] that nature is the opposite of the soul, answering to it part for part. One is seal and one is print. Its beauty is the beauty of his own mind. Its laws are the laws of his own mind. Nature then becomes to him the measure of his attainments. So much of nature as he is ignorant of, so much of his own mind does he not yet possess. And, in fine, the ancient precept, "Know thyself," and the modern precept, "Study nature," become at last one maxim.

II. The next great influence into the spirit of the scholar is the mind of the Past,—in whatever form, whether of literature, of art, of institutions, that mind is inscribed. Books are the best type of the influence of the past, and perhaps we shall get at the truth,—learn the amount of this influence more conveniently,—by considering their value alone.

The theory of books is noble. The scholar of the first age received into him the world around; brooded thereon; gave it the new arrangement of his own mind, and uttered it again. It came into him life; it went out from him truth. It came to him short-lived actions, it went out from him immortal thoughts. It came to him business; it went from him poetry. It was dead fact; now, it is quick thought. It can [88] stand, and it can go. It now endures, it now flies, it now inspires. Precisely in proportion to the depth of mind from which it is-sued, so high does it soar, so long does it sing.

Or, I might say, it depends on how far the process had gone, of transmuting life into truth. In proportion to the completeness of the distillation, so will the purity and imperishableness of the product be. But none is quite perfect. As no air-pump can by any means make a perfect vacuum, so neither can any artist entirely exclude the conventional, the local, the perishable from his book, or write a book of pure thought, that shall be as efficient, in all re-spects, to a remote posterity, as to contemporaries, or rather to the second age. Each age, it is found, must write its own books; or rather, each gen-eration for the next succeeding. The books of an older period will not fit this.

Yet hence arises a grave mischief. The sacredness which attaches to the act of creation, the act of thought, is transferred to the record. The poet chanting was felt to be a divine man: henceforth the chant is divine also. The writer was a just and wise spirit: henceforward it is settled the book is perfect; as love of the hero corrupts into worship of his statue. Instantly [89] the book becomes noxious: the guide is a tyrant. The sluggish and perverted mind of the multitude, slow to open to the incursions of Reason, having once so opened, having once received this book, stands upon it, and makes an outcry if it is disparaged. Colleges are built on it. Books are written on it by thinkers, not by Man Thinking; by men of talent, that is, who start wrong, who set out from accepted dogmas, not from their own sight of principles. Meek young men grow up in libraries, believing it their duty to accept the views which Cicero, which Locke, which Bacon, have given; forgetful that Cicero, Locke, and Bacon were only young men in libraries when they wrote these books.

Hence, instead of Man Thinking, we have the bookworm. Hence the book-learned class, who value books, as such; not as related to nature and the human constitution, but as making a sort of Third Estate with the world and the soul. Hence the restorers of readings, the emendators, the bibliomaniacs of all degrees.

Books are the best of things, well used; abused, among the worst. What is the right use? What is the one end which all means go to effect? They are for nothing but to inspire. I had better [90] never see a book than to be warped by its attraction clean out of my own orbit, and made a satellite instead of a system. The one thing in the world, of value, is the active soul. This every man is entitled to; this every man contains within him, although in almost all men obstructed and as yet unborn. The soul active sees absolute truth and utters truth, or creates. In this action it is genius; not the privilege of here and there a favorite, but the sound estate of every man. In its essence it is progressive. The book, the college, the school of art, the institution of any kind, stop with some past utterance of genius. This is good, say they,—let us hold by this. They pin me down. They look backward and not forward. But genius looks forward: the eyes of man are set in his forehead, not in his hindhead: man hopes: genius creates. Whatever talents may be, if the man create not, the pure efflux of the Deity is not his;—cinders and smoke there may be, but not yet flame. There are creative manners, there are creative actions, and creative words; manners, actions, words, that is, indicative of no custom or authority, but springing spontaneous from the mind's own sense of good and fair.

On the other part, instead of being its own [91] seer, let it receive from another mind its truth, though it were in torrents of light, without periods of solitude, inquest, and self-recovery, and a fatal disservice is done. Genius is always sufficiently the enemy of genius by over-influence. The literature of every nation bears me witness. The English dramatic poets have Shakspear-ized now for two hundred years.

Undoubtedly there is a right way of reading, so it be sternly subordinated. Man Thinking must not be subdued by his instruments. Books are for the scholar's idle times. When he can read God directly, the hour is too precious to be wasted in other men's transcripts of their readings. But when the inter-vals of darkness come, as come they must,—when the sun is hid and the stars withdraw their shining,—we repair to the lamps which were kindled by their ray, to guide our steps to the East again, where the dawn is. We hear, that we may speak. The Arabian proverb says, "A fig tree, looking on a fig tree, becometh fruitful."

It is remarkable, the character of the pleasure we derive from the best books. They impress us with the conviction that one nature wrote and the same reads. We read the verses of one of the great English poets, of Chaucer, of Marvell, [92] of Dryden, with the most modern joy,—with a pleasure, I mean, which is in great part caused by the abstraction of all *time* from their verses. There is some awe mixed with the joy of our surprise, when this poet, who lived in some past world, two or three hundred years ago, says that which lies close to my own soul, that which I also had well-nigh thought and said. But for the evidence thence afforded to the philosophical doctrine of the identity of all minds, we should suppose some preëstablished harmony, some foresight of souls that were to be, and some preparation of stores for their fu-ture wants, like the fact observed in insects, who lay up food-before death for the young grub they shall never see.

I would not be hurried by any love of system, by any exaggeration of in-stincts, to underrate the Book. We all know, that as the human body can be nourished on any food, though it were boiled grass and the broth of shoes, so the human mind can be fed by any knowledge. And great and heroic men have existed who had almost no other information than by the printed page. I only would say that it needs a strong head to bear that diet. One must be an inventor to read well. As the proverb says, "He that would bring home the wealth of the Indies, must [93] carry out the wealth of the Indies." There is then creative reading as well as creative writing. When the mind is braced by labor and invention, the page of whatever book we read becomes luminous with manifold allusion. Every sentence is doubly significant, and the sense of our author is as broad as the world. We then see, what is always true, that as the seer's hour of vision is short and rare among heavy days and months, so is its record, perchance, the least part of his volume. The discerning will read, in his Plato or Shakspeare, only that least part,—only the authentic utterances of the oracle;—all the rest he rejects, were it never so many times Plato's and Shakspeare's.

Of course there is a portion of reading quite indispensable to a wise man. History and exact science he must learn by laborious reading. Colleges, in like manner, have their indispensable office,—to teach elements. But they can only highly serve us when they aim not to drill, but to create; when they gather from far every ray of various genius to their hospitable halls, and by the concentrated fires, set the hearts of their youth on flame. Thought and knowledge are natures in which apparatus and pretension avail nothing. Gowns and pecuniary foundations, [94] though of towns of gold, can never countervail the least sentence or syllable of wit. Forget this, and our American colleges will recede in their public importance, whilst they grow richer every year.

III. There goes in the world a notion that the scholar should be a recluse, a valetudinarian,—as unfit for any handiwork or public labor as a penknife for an axe. The so-called "practical men" sneer at speculative men, as if, because they speculate or *see*, they could do nothing. I have heard it said that the clergy,—who are always, more universally than any other class, the scholars of their day,—are addressed as women; that the rough, spontaneous conversation of men they do not hear, but only a mincing and diluted speech. They are often virtually disfranchised; and indeed there are advocates for their celibacy. As far as this is true of the studious classes, it is not just and wise. Action is with the scholar subordinate, but it is essential. Without it he is not yet man. Without it thought can never ripen into truth. Whilst the world hangs before the eye as a cloud of beauty, we cannot even see its beauty. Inaction is cowardice, but there can be no scholar without the heroic mind. The preamble of thought, the transition [95] through which it passes from the unconscious to the conscious, is action. Only so much do I know, as I have lived. Instantly we know whose words are loaded with life, and whose not.

The world,—this shadow of the soul, or *other me*,—lies wide around. Its attractions are the keys which unlock my thoughts and make me acquainted with myself. I run eagerly into this resounding tumult. I grasp the hands of those next me, and take my place in the ring to suffer and to work, taught by an instinct that so shall the dumb abyss be vocal with speech. I pierce its order; I dissipate its fear; I dispose of it within the circuit of my expanding life. So much only of life as I know by experience, so much of the wilderness have I vanquished and planted, or so far have I extended my being, my dominion. I do not see how any man can afford, for the sake of his nerves and his nap, to spare any action in which he can partake. It is pearls and rubies to his discourse. Drudgery, calamity, exasperation, want, are instructors in eloquence and wisdom. The true scholar grudges every opportunity of action past by, as a loss of power. It is the raw material out of which the intellect moulds her splendid products. [96] A strange process too, this by which experience is converted into thought, as a mulberry leaf is converted into satin. The manufacture goes forward at all hours.

The actions and events of our childhood and youth are now matters of calmest observation. They lie like fair pictures in the air. Not so with our recent actions,—with the business which we now have in hand. On this we are quite unable to speculate. Our affections as yet circulate through it. We no more feel or know it than we feel the feet, or the hand, or the brain of our body. The new deed is yet a part of life,—remains for a time immersed in our unconscious life. In some contemplative hour it detaches itself from the life like a ripe fruit, to become a thought of the mind. Instantly it is raised, transfigured; the corruptible has put on incorruption. Henceforth it is an object of beauty, however base its origin and neighborhood. Observe too the impossibility of antedating this act. In its grub state, it cannot fly, it cannot shine, it is a dull grub. But suddenly, without observation, the selfsame thing unfurls beautiful wings, and is an angel of wisdom. So is there no fact, no event, in our private history, which shall not, sooner or later, lose its [97] adhesive, inert form, and astonish us by soaring from our body into the empyrean. Cradle and infancy, school and playground, the fear of boys, and dogs, and ferules, the love of little maids and berries, and many another fact that once filled the whole sky, are gone already; friend and relative, profession and party, town and country, nation and world, must also soar and sing.

Of course, he who has put forth his total strength in fit actions has the richest return of wisdom. I will not shut myself out of this globe of action, and transplant an oak into a flowerpot, there to hunger and pine; nor trust the revenue of some single faculty, and exhaust one vein of thought, much like those Savoyards, who, getting their livelihood by carving shepherds, shepherdesses, and smoking Dutchmen, for all Europe, went out one day to the mountain to find stock, and discovered that they had whittled up the last of their pine trees. Authors we have, in numbers, who have written out their vein, and who, moved by a commendable prudence, sail for Greece or Palestine, follow the trapper into the prairie, or ramble round Algiers, to replenish their merchantable stock.

If it were only for a vocabulary, the scholar [98] would be covetous of action. Life is our dictionary. Years are well spent in country labors; in town; in the insight into trades and manufactures; in frank intercourse with many men and women; in science; in art; to the one end of mastering in all their facts a language by which to illustrate and embody our perceptions. I learn immediately from any speaker how much he has already lived, through the poverty or the splendor of his speech. Life lies behind us as the quarry from whence we get tiles and copestones for the masonry of to-day. This is the way to learn grammar. Colleges and books only copy the language which the field and the work-yard made.

But the final value of action, like that of books, and better than books, is that it is a resource. That great principle of Undulation in nature, that shows itself in the inspiring and expiring of the breath; in desire and satiety; in the ebb and flow of the sea; in day and night; in the heat and cold; and, as yet more deeply ingrained in every atom and every fluid, is known to us under the name of Polarity,—these "fits of easy transmission and reflection," as Newton called them, are the law of nature because they are the law of spirit.

[99] The mind now thinks, now acts, and each fit reproduces the other. When the artist has exhausted his materials, when the fancy no longer paints, when thoughts are no longer apprehended and books are a weariness,—he has always the resource *to live*. Character is higher than intellect. Thinking is the function. Living is the functionary. The stream retreats to its source. A great soul will be strong to live, as well as strong to think. Does he lack organ or medium to impart his truths? He can still fall back on this elemental force of living them. This is a total act. Thinking is a partial act. Let the grandeur of justice shine in his affairs. Let the beauty of affection cheer his lowly roof. Those "far from fame," who dwell and act with him, will feel the force of his constitution in the doings and passages of the day better than it can be measured by any public and designed display. Time shall teach him that the scholar loses no hour which the man lives. Herein he unfolds the sacred germ

of his instinct, screened from influence. What is lost in seemliness is gained in strength. Not out of those on whom systems of education have exhausted their culture, comes the helpful giant to destroy the old or to build the new, but out of unhandselled [2] [100] savage nature; out of terrible Druids and Berserkers come at last Alfred [3] and Shakspeare.

I hear therefore with joy whatever is beginning to be said of the dignity and necessity of labor to every citizen. There is virtue yet in the hoe and the spade, for learned as well as for unlearned hands. And labor is everywhere welcome; always we are invited to work; only be this limitation observed, that a man shall not for the sake of wider activity sacrifice any opinion to the popular judgments and modes of action.

I have now spoken of the education of the scholar by nature, by books, and by action. It remains to say somewhat of his duties

They are such as become Man Thinking. They may all be comprised in self-trust. The office of the scholar is to cheer, to raise, and to guide men by showing them facts amidst appearances. He plies the slow, unhonored, and unpaid task of observation. Flamsteed and Herschel,[4] in their glazed observatories, may catalogue the stars with the praise of all men, and the results being splendid and useful, honor is sure. But he, in his private observatory, cataloguing obscure and nebulous stars of the human [101] mind, which as yet no man has thought of as such,—watching days and months sometimes for a few facts; correcting still his old records;—must relinquish display and immediate fame. In the long period of his preparation he must betray often an ignorance and shiftlessness in popular arts, incurring the disdain of the able who shoulder him aside. Long he must stammer in his speech; often forego the living for the dead. Worse yet, he must accept—how often!—poverty and solitude. For the ease and pleasure of treading the old road, accepting the fashions, the education, the religion of society, he takes the cross of mak-

---

[2] The original meaning of the archaic word "handsel" was "a lucky gift or sign"; thus "unhandselled" would seem to mean "unlucky" or "unproven." Emerson apparently uses the word in the figurative sense of "unpromising" or "inauspicious."

[3] Druids were priests of ancient Gaul, Britain, and Ireland; berserkers were early Scandinavian warriors of legendary strength and violence; Alfred (849–899) was a famous Saxon king, lawgiver, and writer.

[4] John Flamsteed (1646–1719) was an English astronomer; Emerson may be referring to Sir Frederick William Herschel (1738–1822), who discovered the planet Uranus in 1781, or to his son, Sir John Frederick William Herschel (1792–1871), who was also a renowned English astronomer.

ing his own, and, of course, the self-accusation, the faint heart, the frequent uncertainty and loss of time, which are the nettles and tangling vines in the way of the self-relying and self-directed; and the state of virtual hostility in which he seems to stand to society, and especially to educated society. For all this loss and scorn, what offset? He is to find consolation in exercising the highest functions of human nature. He is one who raises himself from private considerations and breathes and lives on public and illustrious thoughts. He is the world's eye. He is the world's heart. He is to resist the vulgar prosperity that retrogrades [102] ever to barbarism, by preserving and communicating heroic sentiments, noble biographies, melodious verse, and the conclusions of history. Whatsoever oracles the human heart, in all emergencies, in all solemn hours, has uttered as its commentary on the world of actions,—these he shall receive and impart. And whatsoever new verdict Reason from her inviolable seat pronounces on the passing men and events of to-day,—this he shall hear and promulgate.

These being his functions, it becomes him to feel all confidence in himself, and to defer never to the popular cry. He and he only knows the world. The world of any moment is the merest appearance. Some great decorum, some fetish of a government, some ephemeral trade, or war, or man, is cried up by half mankind and cried down by the other half, as if all depended on this particular up or down. The odds are that the whole question is not worth the poorest thought which the scholar has lost in listening to the controversy. Let him not quit his belief that a popgun is a popgun, though the ancient and honorable of the earth affirm it to be the crack of doom. In silence, in steadiness, in severe abstraction, let him hold by himself; add [103] observation to observation, patient of neglect, patient of reproach, and bide his own time,— happy enough if he can satisfy himself alone that this day he has seen something truly. Success treads on every right step. For the instinct is sure, that prompts him to tell his brother what he thinks. He then learns that in going down into the secrets of his own mind he has descended into the secrets of all minds. He learns that he who has mastered any law in his private thoughts, is master to that extent of all men whose language he speaks, and of all into whose language his own can be translated. The poet, in utter solitude remembering his spontaneous thoughts and recording them, is found to have recorded that which men in crowded cities find true for them also. The orator distrusts at first the fitness of his frank confessions, his want of knowledge of the persons he addresses, until he finds that he is the complement of his hearers;—that they drink his words because he fulfils for them their own nature; the deeper he dives into his privatest, secretest presentiment, to his wonder he finds this is the most acceptable, most public, and universally true. The people delight in it; the better part of every man feels, This is my music; this is myself.

[104] In self-trust all the virtues are comprehended. Free should the scholar be,—free and brave. Free even to the definition of freedom, "without any hindrance that does not arise out of his own constitution." Brave; for fear is a thing which a scholar by his very function puts behind him. Fear always springs from ignorance. It is a shame to him if his tranquillity, amid dangerous times, arise from the presumption that like children and women his is a protected class; or if he seek a temporary peace by the diversion of his thoughts from politics or vexed questions, hiding his head like an ostrich in the flowering bushes, peeping into microscopes, and turning rhymes, as a boy whistles to keep his courage up. So is the danger a danger still; so is the fear worse. Manlike let him turn and face it. Let him look into its eye and search its nature, inspect its origin,—see the whelping of this lion,—which lies no great way back; he will then find in himself a perfect comprehension of its nature and extent; he will have made his hands meet on the other side, and can henceforth defy it and pass on superior. The world is his who can see through its pretension. What deafness, what stone-blind custom, what overgrown error you behold is there only by suffer- [105] ance,—by your sufferance. See it to be a lie, and you have already dealt it its mortal blow.

Yes, we are the cowed,—we the trustless. It is a mischievous notion that we are come late into nature; that the world was finished a long time ago. As the world was plastic and fluid in the hands of God, so it is ever to so much of his attributes as we bring to it. To ignorance and sin, it is flint. They adapt themselves to it as they may; but in proportion as a man has any thing in him divine, the firmament flows before him and takes his signet and form. Not he is great who can alter matter, but he who can alter my state of mind. They are the kings of the world who give the color of their present thought to all nature and all art, and persuade men by the cheerful serenity of their carrying the matter, that this thing which they do is the apple which the ages have desired to pluck, now at last ripe, and inviting nations to the harvest. The great man makes the great thing. Wherever Macdonald sits, there is the head of the table.[5] Linnæus makes botany the most alluring of studies, and wins it from the farmer and the herb-woman; Davy, chemistry; and Cuvier, fossils.[6] The day is always his who works in it with serenity and great aims. The unstable estimates [106] of men crowd to him whose mind is filled with a truth, as the heaped waves of the Atlantic follow the moon.

For this self-trust, the reason is deeper than can be fathomed,—darker than can be enlightened. I might not carry with me the feeling of my audience in stating my own belief. But I have already shown the ground of my hope in adverting to the doctrine that man is one. I believe man has been wronged; he has wronged himself. He has almost lost the light that can lead him back to his prerogatives. Men are become of no account. Men in history, men in the world of to-day, are bugs, are spawn, and are called "the mass" and "the herd." In a century, in a millennium, one or two men; that is to say, one or two approximations to the right state of every man. All the rest behold in the hero or the poet their own green and crude being,—ripened; yes, and are content to be less, so *that* may attain to its full stature. What a testimony, full of grandeur, full of pity, is borne to the demands of his own nature, by the poor clansman, the poor partisan, who rejoices in the glory of his chief. The poor and the low find some amends to their immense moral capacity, for their acquiescence in a political and social inferiority. [107] They are content to be brushed like flies from the path of a great person, so that justice shall be done by him to that common nature which it is the dearest desire of all to see enlarged and glorified. They sun themselves in the great man's light, and feel it to be their own element. They cast the dignity of man from their downtrod selves upon the shoulders of a hero, and will perish to add one drop of blood to make that great heart beat, those giant sinews combat and conquer. He lives for us, and we live in him.

Men, such as they are, very naturally seek money or power; and power because it is as good as money,—the "spoils," so called, "of office." And why not? for they aspire to the highest, and this, in their sleep-walking, they dream is highest. Wake them and they shall quit the false good and leap to

[5] This sentence is apparently an aphorism familiar to readers in Emerson's time. Macdonald is the "head of the clan."

[6] Linnaeus, or Carl von Linné (1707–1778), was a Swedish botanist who originated the modern system of nomenclature for botanical species; Sir Humphry Davy (1778–1829) was the English chemist who first prepared potassium and sodium by means of electrolysis; Baron Georges Cuvier (1769–1832) was a French naturalist and comparative anatomist.

the true, and leave governments to clerks and desks. This revolution is to be wrought by the gradual domestication of the idea of Culture. The main enterprise of the world for splendor, for extent, is the upbuilding of a man. Here are the materials strewn along the ground. The private life of one man shall be a more illustrious monarchy, more formidable to its enemy, more sweet and serene in its influence to its friend, than any kingdom in history. For [108] a man, rightly viewed, comprehendeth the particular natures of all men. Each philosopher, each bard, each actor has only done for me, as by a delegate, what one day I can do for myself. The books which once we valued more than the apple of the eye, we have quite exhausted. What is that but saying that we have come up with the point of view which the universal mind took through the eyes of one scribe; we have been that man, and have passed on. First, one, then another, we drain all cisterns, and waxing greater by all these supplies, we crave a better and more abundant food. The man has never lived that can feed us ever. The human mind cannot be enshrined in a person who shall set a barrier on any one side to this unbounded, unboundable empire. It is one central fire, which, flaming now out of the lips of Etna, lightens the capes of Sicily, and now out of the throat of Vesuvius, illuminates the towers and vineyards of Naples. It is one light which beams out of a thousand stars. It is one soul which animates all men.

But I have dwelt perhaps tediously upon this abstraction of the Scholar. I ought not to delay longer to add what I have to say of nearer reference to the time and to this country.

[109] Historically, there is thought to be a difference in the ideas which predominate over successive epochs, and there are data for marking the genius of the Classic, of the Romantic, and now of the Reflective or Philosophical age. With the views I have intimated of the oneness or the identity of the mind through all individuals, I do not much dwell on these differences. In fact, I believe each individual passes through all three. The boy is a Greek; the youth, romantic; the adult, reflective. I deny not, however, that a revolution in the leading idea may be distinctly enough traced.

Our age is bewailed as the age of Introversion. Must that needs be evil? We, it seems, are critical; we are embarrassed with second thoughts; we cannot enjoy any thing for hankering to know whereof the pleasure consists; we are lined with eyes; we see with our feet; the time is infected with Hamlet's unhappiness,—

"Sicklied o'er with the pale cast of thought." [7]

It is so bad then? Sight is the last thing to be pitied. Would we be blind? Do we fear lest we should outsee nature and God, and drink truth dry? I look upon the discontent of the literary class as a mere announcement of the fact [110] that they find themselves not in the state of mind of their fathers, and regret the coming state as untried; as a boy dreads the water before he has learned that he can swim. If there is any period one would desire to be born in, is it not the age of Revolution; when the old and the new stand side by side and admit of being compared; when the energies of all men are searched by fear and by hope; when the historic glories of the old can be compensated by the rich possibilities of the new era? This time, like all times, is a very good one, if we but know what to do with it.

I read with some joy of the auspicious signs of the coming days, as they glimmer already through poetry and art, through philosophy and science, through church and state.

One of these signs is the fact that the same movement which effected the elevation of what was called the lowest class in the state, assumed in literature a very marked and as benign an aspect. Instead of the sublime and beautiful, the near, the low, the common, was explored and poetized. That which had been negligently trodden under foot by those who were harnessing and provisioning themselves for long journeys into far countries, is suddenly found to be richer [111] than all foreign parts. The literature of the poor, the feelings of the child, the philosophy of the street, the meaning of household life, are the topics of the time. It is a great stride. It is a sign—is it not?—of new vigor when the extremities are made active, when currents of warm life run into the hands and the feet. I ask not for the great, the remote, the romantic; what is doing in Italy or Arabia; what is Greek art, or Provençal minstrelsy; I embrace the common, I explore and sit at the feet of the familiar, the low. Give me insight into to-day, and you may have the antique and future worlds. What would we really know the meaning of? The meal in the firkin; the milk

[7] *Hamlet* III.i.85.

in the pan; the ballad in the street; the news of the boat; the glance of the eye; the form and the gait of the body;—show me the ultimate reason of these matters; show me the sublime presence of the highest spiritual cause lurking, as always it does lurk, in these suburbs and extremities of nature; let me see every trifle bristling with the polarity that ranges it instantly on an eternal law; and the shop, the plough, and the ledger referred to the like cause by which light undulates and poets sing;—and the world lies no longer a dull miscellany and lumber-room, [112] but has form and order; there is no trifle, there is no puzzle, but one design unites and animates the farthest pinnacle and the lowest trench.

This idea has inspired the genius of Goldsmith, Burns, Cowper, and, in a newer time, of Goethe, Wordsworth, and Carlyle. This idea they have differently followed and with various success. In contrast with their writing, the style of Pope, of Johnson, of Gibbon, looks cold and pedantic. This writing is blood-warm. Man is surprised to find that things near are not less beautiful and wondrous than things remote. The near explains the far. The drop is a small ocean. A man is related to all nature. This perception of the worth of the vulgar is fruitful in discoveries. Goethe, in this very thing the most modern of the moderns, has shown us, as none ever did, the genius of the ancients.

There is one man of genius who has done much for this philosophy of life, whose literary value has never yet been rightly estimated;—I mean Emanuel Swedenborg.[8] The most imaginative of men, yet writing with the precision of a mathematician, he endeavored to engraft a purely philosophical Ethics on the popular Christianity of his time. Such an attempt of course must have difficulty which no genius [113] could surmount. But he saw and showed the connection between nature and the affections of the soul. He pierced the emblematic or spiritual character of the visible, audible, tangible world. Especially did his shade-loving muse hover over and interpret the lower parts of nature; he showed the mysterious bond that allies moral evil to the foul material forms, and has given in epical parables a theory of insanity, of beasts, of unclean and fearful things.

Another sign of our times, also marked by an analogous political move-

[8] Emanuel Swedenborg (1688–1772) was a Swedish theologian whose thought had much influence on Emerson. He represented the figure of "The Mystic" in Emerson's *Representative Men* (1850).

ment, is the new importance given to the single person. Every thing that tends to insulate the individual,—to surround him with barriers of natural respect, so that each man shall feel the world is his, and man shall treat with man as a sovereign state with a sovereign state,—tends to true union as well as greatness. "I learned," said the melancholy Pestalozzi,[9] "that no man in God's wide earth is either willing or able to help any other man." Help must come from the bosom alone. The scholar is that man who must take up into himself all the ability of the time, all the contributions of the past, all the hopes of the future. He must be an university of knowledges. If there be one lesson more than another which [114] should pierce his ear, it is, The world is nothing, the man is all; in yourself is the law of all nature, and you know not yet how a globule of sap ascends; in yourself slumbers the whole of Reason; it is for you to know all; it is for you to dare all. Mr. President and Gentlemen, this confidence in the unsearched might of man belongs, by all motives, by all prophecy, by all preparation, to the American Scholar. We have listened too long to the courtly muses of Europe. The spirit of the American freeman is already suspected to be timid, imitative, tame. Public and private avarice make the air we breathe thick and fat. The scholar is decent, indolent, complaisant. See already the tragic consequence. The mind of this country, taught to aim at low objects, eats upon itself. There is no work for any but the decorous and the complaisant. Young men of the fairest promise, who begin life upon our shores, inflated by the mountain winds, shined upon by all the stars of God, find the earth below not in unison with these, but are hindered from action by the disgust which the principles on which business is managed inspire, and turn drudges, or die of disgust, some of them suicides. What is the remedy? They did not yet see, and thousands of young men as hopeful [115] now crowding to the barriers for the career do not yet see, that if the single man plant himself indomitably on his instincts, and there abide, the huge world will come round to him. Patience,—patience; with the shades of all the good and great for company; and for solace the perspective of your own infinite life; and for work the study and the communication of principles, the making those instincts prevalent, the conversion of the world. Is it not the chief disgrace in the world, not to be an unit;—not to be reckoned one character;—

---

[9] Johann Heinrich Pestalozzi (1746–1827) was a Swiss educator much admired by the New England Transcendentalists, especially Amos Bronson Alcott, who adopted some of Pestalozzi's principles in his own school.

not to yield that peculiar fruit which each man was created to bear, but to be reckoned in the gross, in the hundred, or the thousand, of the party, the section, to which we belong; and our opinion predicted geographically, as the north, or the south? Not so, brothers and friends—please God, ours shall not be so. We will walk on our own feet; we will work with our own hands; we will speak our own minds. The study of letters shall be no longer a name for pity, for doubt, and for sensual indulgence. The dread of man and the love of man shall be a wall of defence and a wreath of joy around all. A nation of men will for the first time exist, because each believes himself inspired by the Divine Soul which also inspires all men.

QUESTIONS FOR DISCUSSION

Understanding the Text

1. What is the major topic of Emerson's introductory paragraph? How would you describe its tone? Has his prediction about poetry been in any way fulfilled? What is the "pole-star" which guides our age?

2. In the division of man's functions, as they are "parcelled out to individuals" in the social state, what is the scholar's function? What does Emerson mean when he defines the scholar as "Man Thinking"? How is "Man Thinking" distinguished from a thinker in his nature and activities? from an intellectual? from a college student?

3. In discussing the unity of things which appear diverse in nature, Emerson says that natural objects are not chaotic "but have a law which is also a law of the human mind." How does he justify this romantic idea that nature is the counterpart or mirror image of the soul?

4. What does Emerson say about the right use of books? About their abuse? In this discussion he contrasts men of genius and talent. What does he mean by "genius"? How does it differ from talent?

5. What does Emerson mean by "creative reading"? How does it differ from the conventional gathering of information from textbooks? Why does he call the reading of history and science "indispensable" but "laborious"?

6. Commenting on the third major influence on the scholar, Emerson says that "Action is with the scholar subordinate, but it is essential." Later he says that character, which is formed by action or experience, "is higher than intellect." Is there a contradiction in these statements? Is Emerson refusing to choose between the alternatives of contemplation and action in the scholar's life? What is the relation of action to wisdom? To vocabulary?

7. Emerson says that the duties of the scholar "may all be comprised in self-trust." What virtues are encompassed by self-trust? If the scholar is faithful to his duties, what sacrifices must he make? Emerson admonishes the scholar to resist a "vulgar prosperity." Does this view have merit today? Or have the affluent conditions of modern life made the notion of the scholar's "poverty and solitude" somewhat irrelevant? Explain.

31

8. What does Emerson say about the rewards of the scholar's function? Are these rewards greater now than they were in Emerson's time? Explain your answer.

9. According to Emerson the scholar can speak for "the one soul which animates all men." What are the features of this soul as Emerson imagines it? Does such a soul really exist? Is "soul" a metaphor for something else? What sort of man does a scholar have to be in order to serve as spokesman for this soul?

10. Did Emerson expect the American scholar to take sides in great controversies? What evidence do you find for your answer? What were some of the great issues of Emerson's time? What did he dissent against? Does the essay suggest whether his dissent would be moderate or militant? Explain. Useful information can be obtained from the sources listed in the "Bibliographical Suggestions" and from social or political histories such as Alice Felt Tyler, *Freedom's Ferment* (New York: Harper Torchbooks, 1962), pp. 308–350, 396–462, 513–547; Nelson M. Blake, *A Short History of American Life* (New York: McGraw-Hill, 1952), pp. 268–293; Oscar Handlin, *The Americans* (Boston: Little, Brown and Co., 1963), pp. 224–237.

11. What evidence do you find in the essay of Emerson's training and early experience as a minister? In what respects are his language and thought religious?

12. How is Emerson's essay organized? Do its ideas have a meaningful development and progression? Write a topic (or sentence) outline of the essay.

Evaluating Ideas

1. After announcing the subject of his essay, Emerson describes the fable of Man divided into men. What does he say about the specialist or functionary as opposed to "the whole man" or the idea of Man? Is it possible in the modern world of accumulated knowledge for the individual to achieve the condition of the whole man? If so, how can this condition be accomplished?

2. Turning directly to the scholar, "in his school," Emerson considers the three major influences on him. "What is nature to him?" Emerson asks, referring to the first and, in his view, the most important of these influences. A year earlier, in his little book called *Nature* (1836), Emerson explained that in "enumerating the values of nature," he customarily used the term "nature" in both its philosophical and common meanings. "Philosophically considered," he wrote, "the universe is composed of Nature and the Soul. Strictly speaking, therefore, all that is separate from us, all which Philosophy distinguishes as the NOT ME, that is, both nature and art, all other men and my own body, must be ranked under this name, NATURE." (Emerson's friend Thomas Carlyle used the terms ME and NOT ME in *Sartor Resartus* in 1836. The distinction, like Emerson's, is between the self and nonself.) "*Nature*, in the

common sense," Emerson continued, "refers to essences unchanged by man; space, the air, the river, the leaf." (He had no notion, of course, of the remarkable changes that future generations would make in space, or the awful havoc they would wreak on the air, the river, and the forest.) In the same book, Emerson defined "art" as the mixture of man's will with nature so as to produce, with "a little chipping, baking, patching, and washing," such things as "a house, a canal, a statue, a picture."

Now consider again Emerson's question about the scholar: "What is nature to him?" How does Emerson answer it? Is he using the word "nature" here in its philosophical or common sense, or both? Considering yourself as the American scholar, what is nature to you? Do you have some sense of emanating from nature or being a part of nature? Or is nature something separate from you? If so, is its influence beneficent, indifferent, or hostile? Explain.

3. In a letter written in 1835 to his future wife, Lydia Jackson, Emerson described himself as "born a poet," though he usually wrote prose. "Still am I a poet," he said, "in the sense of a perceiver and dear lover of the harmonies that are in the soul and in matter, and especially of the correspondences between these and those." What is the relation of this poetic view and his assumption in "The American Scholar" that studying nature is the same as knowing one's self?

4. Summarize Emerson's theory of books. Why must each generation write its own books? What dangers lie in the uncritical acceptance of books? Can you give any examples from history of an unreasoning faith in particular books? Emerson seems to be thinking of his audience of college students when he speaks of meek young men in libraries. Is this an accurate description of today's college students? Explain. What does Emerson mean by "bibliomaniacs"? What is his quarrel with them? Is it justified? Explain.

5. What, according to Emerson, is the "indispensable office" of the college? Do you agree with his view? Emerson warns that while American colleges grow richer every year, they may "recede in public importance." Can you give examples of this, or have American colleges avoided this danger?

6. Emerson seems especially sensitive about the importance of action, since the scholar in the nineteenth century was often criticized because of his intellectual preoccupation. How does Emerson describe society's typical criticism of the scholar? How would you describe society's regard for the scholar today? In what respects has it changed since Emerson's day?

7. Emerson characterizes his own time as an age of reflection and of revolution. What "auspicious signs of the coming days" does he see? What advantages does he find in living in an age of change and revolution? Do you agree that we are now living in a comparable period of social revolution? If so, what are some of the contemporary signs of revolution? What advantages or disadvantages do you find in living during such a time?

8. What is the subject of Emerson's conclusion to his essay? Does his confidence in the power of the American scholar seem justified, or is it a romantic exaggeration of the scholar's potential influence? Does his charge that the scholar is "decent, indolent, complaisant" seem true today? If not, what are some of the ways in which the scholar has overcome his complaisance? Are current social and academic upheavals a result of "the study and the communication of principles" and the willingness to "speak our own minds"? Does Emerson's comment that "the dread of man and the love of man shall be a wall of defence and a wreath of joy around all" have a modern ring? In what way?

9. In a lecture on education written three months before "The American Scholar," Emerson remarked that the religion, politics, and literature of the time revealed a "great hollowness." "A desperate conservatism clings with both hands to every dead form in the schools, in the state, in the church," he wrote. How are these sentiments treated in "The American Scholar"? Are they relevant today? Explain.

10. In various places in "The American Scholar" Emerson repudiates the widely accepted view that the scholar should be the product of traditional social and educational influences. He distrusts the institutional nurture of the scholar and argues for the influence of nature, self-reliance, and primary experience. Support your agreement or disagreement with his position. In what respects are campus rebellions today a consequence of the stereotyped practices of educational institutions trying to nurture the American scholar in traditional institutional ways? What are some of these institutional ways and how do they obstruct the growth of the scholar? Emerson's own transcendental views and faith in self-reliance were much influenced by his earnest reading in Oriental religion, philosophy, and literature. Is the current student interest in Oriental thought, mysticism, Zen, transcendental meditation, yoga, and occult knowledge an expression of the desire for self-reliance and primary experience? Explain your answer.

CRITICAL VIEWS OF
"THE AMERICAN SCHOLAR"

EMERSON'S MOST FAMOUS SPEECH

Bliss Perry

Bliss Perry was a novelist, editor and critic. During his long tenure on the Harvard English faculty he was known to generations of students as one of the most inspiring teachers in America. His *Emerson Today* (1931) is still a good introduction to the study of Emerson's writings.

I

[81] LET US go upon a literary pilgrimage. The shrine which we are to visit is sacred in the memory of scholars, although Mr. Howells, with dispassionate candor, once described it as the ugliest spot in the universe of God. It is Harvard Square. Eighty-six years ago—or, to be precise, on August 31, 1837, Phi Beta Kappa day—it was not without a certain tranquil, rural beauty. Great elms shadowed the little green, in whose center stood a town pump quite after the taste of Hawthorne—although very few Phi Beta Kappa men chose to utilize it on anniversary days, to the scandal of the water-drinking minority. Northwestward from the Square runs the broad road to Lexington and Concord, and on the left, opposite the low-fenced Harvard Yard, is the meeting-house of the First Parish. This edifice, completed in 1834, was the successor of that log meeting-house where just two hundred years before, in the summer of 1637, Anne Hutchinson had been brought to trial by the New England Theocracy, and condemned to exile. If any ghosts of the past are hovering in the First Parish Church on this August morning of 1837, [82] surely among them is the amused ghost of that clever woman, waiting to see what will happen to a new champion of rebellion.

Here, then, is our shrine, a plain wooden meeting-house in a country village, built big enough for the modest needs of Harvard University on its anniversary occasions. Let us march toward it in the procession of our Phi Beta

From Bliss Perry, *The Praise of Folly and Other Papers* (Boston and New York: Houghton Mifflin Company, 923), pp. 81–113. Reprinted by permission of the publisher.

Kappa brethren, two hundred and fifteen strong, starting at twelve o'clock precisely from University Hall, in the middle of the Harvard Yard. Preceded by a band of music and the dark-gowned undergraduate members, the black-coated double file of graduate members emerge from the Yard, cross the road —the dust has been laid by the unwonted rain of the previous day—and halt in front of the meeting-house. The undergraduates open to the right and left, and the President of Phi Beta Kappa, the secretary, chaplain, orator, and poet enter in that order, followed by the members, two and two, according to seniority. Brother John Pierce, D.D., of Brookline (Harvard, 1793), indefatigable attendant and notetaker of Harvard anniversaries, will describe the occasion—an epoch-making occasion, although he did not suspect it.

For, let me warn you, before quoting his record of Phi Beta Kappa's most famous day, that the [83] excellent Brother Pierce has a blind spot in those shrewd old eyes of his, and that his mind is beautifully fortified against doctrines which he disapproves. In that unhappy division of the Congregational churches which had absorbed so much of the attention of New England for thirty years, Dr. Pierce stands for Orthodoxy, and year by year, at Harvard Commencements, he has found himself in an ever-diminishing minority. He computes the reckoning annually, and only yesterday, on August 30, 1837, he has discovered that among Harvard graduates in the active ministry there are one hundred and twelve Liberals to but fifty-one of the Orthodox. Like every true New Englander, no doubt, he felt that the growing unpopularity of his opinions was the best confirmation of their soundness. His passion for oratory never abated, though he lived to attend sixty-four Commencements, but from the beginning to the end of his career, Brother Pierce was suspicious of every intellectual or spiritual novelty.

Aside from this air-tight characteristic of the good man's mind, he is an admirable critic. He sums up Brother Pipon's Phi Beta Kappa Oration of 1803 in one line: it "consisted of miscellaneous and severely critical remarks on Man." I seem to have heard Brother Pipon's oration myself! Dr. Pierce usually characterizes the prayers with [84] which the Phi Beta Kappa ceremonies opened. They are "appropriate," or "pertinent," or "pertinent and judicious," or, at least, "4 minutes" long, or "12½ minutes" long; but I regret to say that, in 1804, when Emerson's father—a well-known Liberal—acted as chaplain, Brother Pierce contented himself by recording: "Dr. Emerson then prayed." In 1836 he is still watching the chaplain with the ear of a heresy-hunter: "The Rev. George Ripley [Harvard, 1823] offered an elaborate prayer of 13 minutes, elegantly composed and expressed. In my mind it was deficient in not giving sufficient prominence to the name which is above every name." Dr. Pierce's instinct was justified by the event: two years later, George Ripley will be found defending Emerson's "Divinity School Address"!

The good Doctor, in short, had, like all of us, the defects of his qualities, as a listener to poetry and oratory. He confesses it with admirable frankness. In 1811 he notes: "John Stickney, Esquire, delivered an oration, of three quarters of an hour, on The Qualifications of a Statesman. Through the course of it I reproached myself with the obtuseness of my faculties, as there was so large a portion of it of which I could not form the trace of a conception. But upon mentioning my [85] difficulty to intelligent men, I found that I was not alone. In short, I could compare it to nothing more striking than a dark night now and then enlightened by flashes of lightning."

In 1818, according to Brother Pierce, Caleb Cushing delivers a Phi Beta Kappa poem "on I cannot tell what." In 1821 the poem by Willian C. Bryant, Esq., "was in Spenserian measure and contained some fine passages. But I was unable to discern a unity of design or precision of subject. It was 25 minutes long." Brother Pierce had, at any rate, an excellent watch! In 1833 he notes: "Prof. Longfellow, of Bowdoin College, gave a poem, I know not on what subject, of 28 minutes. He is a young, handsome man, son of Hon. Stephen Longfellow, Portland, Harvard University, 1798."

II

BUT while you and I have thus been lingering over the mental peculiarities of the Reverend Doctor John Pierce, the black-coated procession is pushing steadily into the crowded church, and up the aisles to the seats of honor. As the band plays its opening voluntary, you may look, if you like, upon the captains of Israel in their high places. There is President Josiah Quincy (Harvard, 1790), a vigorous gentleman of sixty-five; [86] the fire of his youthful congressional eloquence already half forgotten.

Among the Fellows of the Harvard Corporation, you will note two of the foremost lawyers of the Commonwealth, Joseph Story and Lemuel Shaw. Among the Overseers one seeks instinctively for the well-known faces of John Quincy Adams, and the great Dr. Channing and the "Godlike" Daniel Webster. No need to point out the last, in any assembly of New Englanders; you have but to follow the eyes of the crowd. But perhaps these Overseers are absent to-day—since the Phi Beta Kappa orator is only a stickit-minister from

Concord, author of an anonymous, unintelligible, and unsold little book on "Nature"!

The Faculty .of Harvard College are no doubt in their places, as in duty bound, unwearied by the prolonged Commencement exercises of the previous day. The last name upon the Faculty list this year is that of the half-crazed, half-inspired tutor of Greek, Jones Very, of Salem, poet, who is known to idolize the orator. There are "the stern old war gods" of the Divinity School, the Henry Wares, father and son, and J. G. Palfrey, who a year later are to shake their heads in awful but belated protest against Waldo Emerson's astounding utterance to their own pupils, in their very chapel. There is Andrews [87] Norton, now retired from his professorship to the watchful leisure of Shady Hill. Just twenty years ago, as Librarian of Harvard College, he had allowed "Emerson 4th" of the Freshman class, "President Kirkland's Freshman"—a sedate, silent youth—to draw the books of Hume and Priestley and other eighteenth-century thinkers; and here is that very Freshman ready now to utter doctrines which Andrews Norton is soon to characterize as "The Latest Form of Infidelity." Let the Wares and the Nortons listen closely this noon; if they do, they will at least be qualified to say in 1838: "I told you so! I knew it, when I heard his Phi Beta Kappa address!"

But amid all the learning and fashion and beauty which throng the meeting-house, do not overlook the eager boys—for their ears catch overtones and undertones which are unperceived by their elders. You will find two or three Cambridge boys whom you know; one a handsome dreamy Senior who had made an eloquent Coleridgian graduating speech the day before, young Richard H. Dana, home for a year now after his "Two Years Before the Mast"; the other is a reckless, irreverent Junior—not yet exiled to Concord by the Faculty—James Russell Lowell. One Concord boy, we may be sure, is here: grave David Henry Thoreau,[1] graduated yesterday, and [88] fairly certain to celebrate his new liberty by going blackberrying to-day, were it not for his desire to hear a fellow townsman speak. You will recognize, perhaps, among the alumni members of Phi Beta Kappa, the high-bred face of a young Boston lawyer, without clients and reputed to be without ambition, who, nevertheless, within four months of this day and by a single impromptu speech will win his place in the front rank of American orators—Brother Wendell Phil-

---

[1] Although he was christened David Henry, the name Perry uses here, Thoreau reversed the names when he grew to maturity.

lips, of the class of 1831. And there is a garrulous Boston Sophomore who ought to be here—Edward Everett Hale; yet if he had been there he would surely have talked about it to the end of his days, and I cannot remember that he ever mentioned it. Probably he was swapping stories outside the church.

And now the music of the brass band blares out into silence at last, and the great audience hushes itself. The Reverend Mr. Rogers of Boston offers a prayer which wins the full approval of Brother Pierce, being "singularly devout, short and appropriate." Then, introduced by the President of the Society, rises the speaker of the day.

Let us look at him as he was then—and with the eyes of that audience— not as we know him now in marble and bronze, gleaming with the serene light of earthly immortality. He is a tall, [89] thin man of thirty-four, with sloping shoulders, a man born, you would say, like his ancestors for seven generations, to wear black. His face is asymmetrical. Seen from one side, it is that of a shrewd New England farmer; from the other, it is a face of a seer, a

"Prophetic soul of the wide world
Dreaming on things to come."

The cheeks are fresh-colored, like those of all the Emersons. The thin hair is brown. The eyes are deep blue, with violet lights. He stoops a trifle as he arranges his manuscript upon the pulpit. His manner, though slightly constrained, is suave and courteous. No one in that church, as the Reverend Mr. Emerson pronounces the conventional words "Mr. President and Gentlemen," doubts for a moment his ability to deliver an acceptable discourse. Indeed, he had delivered the Phi Beta Kappa poem, three years before. He belonged, as Dr. Holmes said afterward, to the academic races. This is no amateur, but a professional.

As his clear sweet voice enunciates decorously his opening sentences, the elder Bostonians present are reminded, no doubt, of his father, the gifted minister of the First Church, whose premature death in 1811 had left his boys for a while to the charity of the parish. Chief Justice Shaw, there [90] among the Overseers, had boarded with the widow Emerson on Beacon Street, while she was trying to educate her boys in the Latin School, and perhaps the Justice remembers at this moment the clever poem on Liberty which little Waldo had written in that winter of 1815. Judge Shaw has kept it, and the manuscript is in the Harvard Library to-day.

Possibly the memories of the still older generation go back to the speaker's grandfather, the Reverend William Emerson of Concord, patriot chaplain in the Revolution, and a beautiful pulpit orator, like all that tribe. One listener, I am sure, is thinking of the grandfather, namely, old Dr. Ezra Ripley, of Concord (Harvard, 1776), who had married the chaplain's widow and succeeded him as master of the Old Manse, where the little Emerson boys had spent their vacations with their grandmother. Tough old Ezra Ripley is eighty-six now, but he can still drive himself to Cambridge in his sulky, and it will be some years yet before Waldo Emerson will write his obituary and Hawthorne move into the empty Manse. We know now what Emerson thought of him, but I wish I knew what the old champion of Orthodoxy thinks of Emerson as he sits there in the front pew, revolving many things in his kindly heart.

[91] I fancy that the Harvard professors watch the speaker with a curious and perhaps patronizing interest. He owed them little enough. Kirkland, who had been so kind to him in Wadsworth House, is gone, broken before the time. But there sits Professor Edward Tyrrel Channing ("Ned Channing"), who had corrected Emerson's college themes, and Professor Everett, who had set him an elaborate, and for a while a compelling, pattern for public utterance. And, indeed, the boy had won Bowdoin prizes for essays and a Boylston prize for declamation. But he had otherwise gained no distinction in College, had been the seventh choice of his classmates for the position of Class Poet, and was graduated with a rank of thirtieth in a class of fifty-nine. He was not even, in College, a member of Phi Beta Kappa! His younger brothers, Edward and Charles, won that honor easily. Perhaps there are born candidates for Phi Beta Kappa—as some boys are born to bring flowers to the school-teacher; indeed, the "Harvard Advocate" suggested not long ago that the boy who brings flowers to the teacher becomes naturally a Phi Beta Kappa man. It is the old story: Christopher Wordsworth wins all the prizes at Trinity College, Cambridge, while William Wordsworth reads "Clarissa" during the week preceding the examinations, and barely gets a [92] degree. Both Christopher and William have their reward.

If the professors in Harvard College looked askance at Emerson that day, surely the professors of the Divinity School could have done no less. Ask Pro-

fessor Henry Ware, Senior, who had "approbated" Emerson to preach, at the
end of a broken and disappointing career in the Divinity School. "If they had
examined me," said Emerson afterward, "they never would have passed me."
Professor Henry Ware the younger had been Emerson's colleague in the pas-
torate of the Second Church in Boston. There, too, had been failure—as the
world counts failure: a decorous performance of duty for a brief period, ending in an irreconcilable difference of opinion between pastor and people re-
garding the celebration of the communion, and in the pastor's resignation. Ill-
ness and private sorrow had been added to professional chagrin: his young
wife had died; he had sought change and rest in Europe; he had returned
and settled down in Concord to make a scanty living by lecturing and occa-
sional preaching. Sorrow still waylaid him; robbed him of these two brilliant
prize-winning brothers, Edward and Charles. But he had pulled himself together, being of the old unbeatable Puritan stuff; he had married again, had
bought a house, had [93] published a little book, had backed himself to win
against his generation—against the world; and here he is, a sweet-faced, tran-
quil-voiced man, facing the most distinguished audience that could then be
gathered in America, to annunciate his new vision of the eternal Truth. What
are his chances of triumphing? I do not believe that his friend Henry Ware,
Jr., much as he liked Emerson personally, thought that he had one chance in
a thousand. But we talk too much about chances: one chance is enough, if
you have the right moment and the man. "All that a man ought to ask for in
life," said the French etcher Méryon, "is the chance to put himself into his
plates." That supreme felicity was Emerson's, in that August noontide of long
ago. He put himself into the oration on "The American Scholar."

I do not say that he won everybody in that packed meeting-house. Certainly he did not convince our hard-headed Brother John Pierce, sitting there
on a front seat immovable and unconvincible—watch in hand. Listen to his
impression of the address; but listen respectfully, for he is an honest man, and
he utters the verdict of the older generation:

Rev. Ralph Waldo Emerson gave an oration, of 1¼ hour, on The American
Scholar. It was to me in the misty, dreamy, unintelligible style of Swedenborg, [94]
Coleridge, and Carlyle. He professed to have method; but I could not trace it, except
in his own annunciation. It was well spoken, and all seemed to attend, but how
many were in my own predicament of making little of it I have no means of ascer-
taining. Toward the close, and indeed in many parts of his discourse, he spoke se-

verely of our dependence on British literature. Notwithstanding, I much question whether he himself would have written such an apparently incoherent and unintelligible address, had he not been familiar with the writings of the authors above named. He had already, in 1834, delivered a poem before the Society.

And now farewell to Brother Pierce—though he lives to attend eleven more meetings of the Society. The good man had his chance, too!

III

I MUST call three other witnesses to the effect of the oration, familiar to many of you as their testimony may be. Let us hear first a clever young Boston doctor, son of the minister of the First Church in Cambridge and brought up in its gambrel-roofed parsonage. He was the pet and the glory of the class of 1829. He had delighted the Phi Beta Kappa Society with his poem in 1836. He is not yet the "Autocrat," but he knows his own mind and the mind of the younger generation. Oliver Wendell Holmes testifies:

[95] This grand Oration was our intellectual Declaration of Independence. Nothing like it had been heard in the halls of Harvard since Samuel Adams supported the affirmative of the question, "Whether it be lawful to resist the chief magistrate, if the commonwealth cannot otherwise be preserved." It was easy to find fault with an expression here and there. The dignity, not to say the formality of an Academic assembly was startled by the realism that looked for the infinite in "the meal in the firkin; the milk in the pan." They could understand the deep thoughts suggested by "the meanest flower that blows," but these domestic illustrations had a kind of nursery homeliness about them which the grave professors and sedate clergymen were unused to expect on so stately an occasion. But the young men went out from it as if a prophet had been proclaiming to them "Thus saith the Lord." No listener ever forgot that Address, and among all the noble utterances of the speaker it may be questioned if one ever contained more truth in language more like that of immediate inspiration. . . .

Let us next call to the witness stand that other Cambridge boy whom we have already noted in the audience—the reckless, irreverent "Jamie" Lowell of 1837; sober enough now, when he gives his testimony, and it is the testimony, you will remember, of one of the few genuine critics whom America has produced:

The Puritan revolt had made us ecclesiastically and the Revolution politically independent, but we were socially and intellectually moored to English thought, [96] till Emerson cut the cable and gave us a chance at the dangers and glories of blue water. No man young enough to have felt it can forget or cease to be grateful for the mental and moral *nudge* which he received from the writings of his high-minded and brave-spirited countryman. . . . His oration before the Phi Beta Kappa Society at Cambridge, some thirty years ago, was an event without any former parallel in our literary annals, a scene to be always treasured in the memory for its picturesqueness and its inspiration. What crowded and breathless aisles, what windows clustering with eager heads, what enthusiasm of approval, what grim silence of foregone dissent! It was our Yankee version of a lecture by Abélard, our Harvard parallel to the last public appearances of Schelling. . . .

Finally, lest you may think that the mere spell of the orator's spoken word charmed such hearers as Holmes and Lowell into an unreasoning discipleship, listen to an opinion from across the water, by a Scotchman who called no man, save Goethe, master, and who read Emerson's speech in the vast solitude of London town. Thomas Carlyle wrote:

My friend! You know not what you have done for me there. It was long decades of years that I heard nothing but the infinite jangling and jabbering, and inarticulate twittering and screeching, and my soul had sunk down sorrowful, and said there is no articulate speaking then any more, and thou art solitary among stranger-creatures? and lo, out of the West comes a [97] clear utterance, clearly recognizable as a *man's* voice, and I *have* a kinsman and brother: God be thanked for it! I could have *wept* to read that speech; the clear high melody of it went tingling through my heart; I said to my wife, "There, woman!" She read; and returned, and charges me to return for answer, "that there has been nothing met with like it since Schiller went silent." My brave Emerson! And all this has been lying silent, quite tranquil in him, these seven years, and the "vociferous platitude," dinning his ears on all sides, and he quietly answering no word; and a whole world of Thought has silently built itself in these calm depths, and, the day being come, says quite softly, as if it were a common thing, "Yes, I *am* here too." Miss Martineau tells me, "Some say it is inspired, some say it is mad." Exactly so; no *say* could be suitabler. But for you, my dear friend, I say and pray heartily: may God grant you strength; for you have a *fearful* work to do! Fearful I call it; and yet it is great, and the greatest.

IV

Many readers still imagine that Emerson's address had the advantage of a new theme. It did not. His subject, "The American Scholar," had been a conventional theme of Phi Beta Kappa orations ever since he was a boy. The records of the Harvard Chapter prove this fact, beyond dispute. In 1809, for example, the eloquent Dr. J. S. Buckminster, of Boston, had spoken on the

"Dangers and Duties of Men of Letters"; an [98] admirable moralistic discussion of the infirmities and temptations of the scholastic life, closing with a plea for increased endowments for Harvard. That was his solution of the difficulty!

In 1815, William Tudor, the editor of the newly founded "North American Review," had discussed the "subjects which America would furnish for future poets." This was a favorite topic for Tudor and his associate Walter Channing in the early volumes of the "North American"; and the burden of their argument was that the remedy for American deficiencies lay in a more vigorous exertion of our own minds.

In 1818, at the end of Emerson's Freshman year, Edward Tyrrel Channing, then commencing his long and fruitful career as a Harvard teacher of rhetoric, took for his Phi Beta Kappa theme, "Independence in Literary Pursuits."

In 1822, William J. Spooner, addressing the Society on "The Prospects of American Literature," admitted that all our literature, up to that date, was an English literature, and yet claimed that our literary destiny was to be as independent of England's as was our political and moral destiny. America, he maintains, has already given proofs of "the unconquerable mind"; now, "let our writers learn to think for themselves." Yet Mr. Spooner's peroration, like Dr. Buckminster's, [99] emphasizes the necessity of enlarging the means of education and of raising the standards of scholarship—the old appeal, you will perceive, to Harvard men.

In 1824 came Edward Everett's oration, delivered in the presence of Lafayette and dedicated to him, on "The Peculiar Motives to Intellectual Exertion in America." Those of you to whom Everett's name has not become as shadowy as the names of Tudor and Buckminster will still read this speech with admiration. He uses the very words, "American scholar"; he pleads nobly for popular institutions, for "the manifold brotherhood which unites and will unite the growing millions of America." He sees in vision the vast populations of the Mississippi and Missouri valleys, waiting to be stirred and inspired by the American idea; and his peroration is not a plea for endowments for Harvard, but a welcome to Lafayette. Thus the years come and go with the Harvard Chapter, but the orators pound imperturbably away on the same note! In 1831, it is James T. Austin, on "The Character and Duties of Educated Men." In 1835, we have Judge Theophilus Parsons, "On the Duties of Educated Men in a Republic"—and an excellent standpat speech it is: pleading for the sovereignty of Truth, the sacredness of Law, the security of Property; [100] and President Wayland, of Brown University, the orator of 1836, made much the same plea under another title. In fact, such discussions of the duties and opportunities of the American Scholar were not confined to academic occasions. In 1831, Dr. William Ellery Channing had printed in the "Christian Examiner" his famous article on "National Literature." "In an age of great intellectual activity," he maintains, "we rely chiefly for intellectual excitement and enjoyment on foreign minds; nor is our own mind felt abroad. . . . We believe that a literature springing up in this new soil would bear new fruits. . . . Juster and profounder views of man may be expected here than elsewhere. In Europe political and artificial distinctions have, more or less, triumphed over and obscured our common nature. . . . Man is not hidden from us by so many disguises as in the Old World. . . ." Yet, as a means toward securing this new and native literature, Dr. Channing recommends "to our educated men a more extensive acquaintance with the intellectual labors of Continental Europe. Our reading is confined too much to English books, and especially to the more recent publications of Great Britain." Quickened by this contact with the Continental mind, power will pass increasingly, not into the hands of government, but into the hands of those [101] who think and write. Thomas Carlyle, in that very year, was dreaming the same flattering dream.

You will thus perceive that when the Reverend R. W. Emerson announced in 1837 that his subject was to be "The American Scholar," the Cambridge audience could settle back comfortably in their seats, knowing pretty well what was coming—as you and I do when we listen to a Christmas or an Easter sermon. And I do not need to add that the comfortable Cambridge audience guessed wrong.

V

WHAT was it, after all, that Emerson said, upon his hackneyed theme? What was it that puzzled the elders, and entranced the youth, and sowed the seeds of division? At the Phi Beta Kappa dinner in University Hall, following the exercises in the church—a dinner too Bacchanalian, alas, for the taste of Brother John Pierce—Emerson was toasted in these words: "Mr. President, I suppose you all know where the orator came from; and I suppose all know what he said. I give you—the Spirit of Concord—*it makes us all of one mind.*" The pun was clever enough—as Phi Beta Kappa dinners go—but the well-meant compliment went very wide of the truth. Far from making them all of one mind, the man from [102] Concord had sowed discord—and Emerson, at least, knew it. At the Phi Beta Kappa dinner of the next year, he is aware, his Journal tells us, of the "averted faces," and the aversion dated from this very 31st of August, 1837—it had only ripened by the summer of 1838 and the "Divinity School Address." What had he really uttered in this speech, which was no loving-cup, but a sword?

He had begun with decorous sentences, quiet and clear as the daylight. His very subject, he admits, is prescribed by the occasion. But before one knows it, he is making his first distinction, namely, that Man, in being divided into Men, has suffered, has become a thing—a farmer, let us say, instead of Man on the farm. Now the Scholar should be *Man Thinking*, not a mere thinker, or still worse, the parrot of other men's thinking. What are the influences which the scholar receives?

There are three main influences: Nature, the Past—typified by Books—and Action.

First, then, Nature. "Every day, the sun; and, after sunset, Night and her stars. Ever the winds blow; ever the grass grows." But the scholar must ask what all this means. What *is* Nature? And then comes the puzzling Emersonian answer, already expressed in that little blue-covered unsold [103] book of the year before: Nature is the opposite of the soul, answering to it part for part. (I can fancy Brother John Pierce looking at his watch. Ten minutes gone, and is this nonsense about Nature what we came into the meeting-house to hear?)

But the orator, after these cryptic paragraphs about Nature, is already touching the second influence upon the spirit of the scholar—namely, the Past, or, let us say for convenience, Books. (I imagine that Brother Pierce looks relieved. Books? He has been hearing Phi Beta Kappa talk about books for forty years. It is a safe subject. And yet what is it that the minister from Concord seems to be saying now?) The theory of books is noble, but each age must write its own books. It is the act of creation that is sacred, not the record. The poet chanting was felt to be a divine man: henceforth the chant is divine also. Instantly the book becomes noxious; the guide is a tyrant, though colleges are built on it. (Can he mean the Bible, wonders Professor Ware? Yes, Professor Ware, he does mean the Bible, and he will say so in your own Divinity School upon the invitation of your own students, on the fifteenth of

July next! Listen to him as he goes on!) The one thing in the world, of value, is the active soul. The book, the college, the institution of any kind, [104] stop with some past utterance of genius. This is good, say they—let us hold by this. *They pin me down.* They look backward and not forward. Books are for the scholar's idle times. They serve us best when they aim, not to drill, but to create—when they set the hearts of youth on flame. (I should like to watch Professor Ned Channing's sarcastic face, as Waldo Emerson proclaims this doctrine: Waldo Emerson, who had proved himself in college neither drillable nor inflammable!)

But the imperturbable orator of the day has now reached the third section of his address—a plea for Action. Remember that we are in the golden and serious age of American Rhetoric, and do not smile when Emerson argues that action enriches the scholar's vocabulary! It is pearls and rubies to his discourse! Life is our dictionary. But action is after all better than books. Character is higher than intellect. Thinking is a partial act. The scholar loses no hour which the man lives. Labor is sacred. There is virtue yet in the hoe and the spade even in unlearned hands. (I catch grave young Henry Thoreau smiling a little as Mr. Emerson utters this wholesome New England doctrine of manual labor;—for he has watched the minister trying to spade his new Concord garden, and making but a sorry job of it!)

[105] It remains, concludes the speaker, to say something of the scholar's duties. They may all be comprised in self-trust. Let him not quit his belief that a pop-gun is a pop-gun, though the ancient and honorable of the earth affirm it to be the crack of doom. Let him be free and brave. The world is still fluid, still alive. *Men* count—not "the mass"—"the herd." The private life is the true kingdom. Act for yourself: the man has never lived that can feed us ever. (Professor Ware—stout old war-horse—pricks up his ears again!) But now the orator is sweeping on to this climax: This age of Revolution in which we are living is a very good age. Accept it: embrace the common, the familiar, the low. Burns and Wordsworth and Carlyle are right. Give me insight into to-day, and you may have the antique and future worlds. The important thing is the *single person. The man is all.*

Then follows the wonderful peroration, which you would never forgive me for not quoting word for word:

. . . Mr. President and Gentlemen, this confidence in the unsearched might of man belongs, by all motives, by all prophecy, by all preparation, to the American

Scholar. We have listened too long to the courtly muses of Europe. The spirit of the American freeman is already suspected to be timid, imitative, tame: [106] Public and private avarice make the air we breathe thick and fat. The scholar is decent, indolent, complaisant. See already the tragic consequence. The mind of this country, taught to aim at low objects, eats upon itself. There is no work for any but the decorous and the complaisant. Young men of the fairest promise, who begin life upon our shores, inflated by the mountain winds, shined upon by all the stars of God, find the earth below not in unison with these, but are hindered from action by the disgust which the principles on which business is managed inspire, and turn drudges, or die of disgust, some of them suicides. What is the remedy? They did not yet see, and thousands of young men as hopeful now crowding to the barriers for the career do not yet see, that if the single man plant himself indomitably on his instincts, and there abide, the huge world will come round to him. Patience—patience; with the shades of all the good and great for company; and for solace the perspective of your own infinite life; and for work the study and the communication of principles, the making those instincts prevalent, the conversion of the world. Is it not the chief disgrace in the world, not to be an unit;—not to be reckoned one character;—not to yield that peculiar fruit which each man was created to bear, but to be reckoned in the gross, in the hundred, or the thousand, of the party, the section, to which we belong; and our opinion predicted geographically, as the north, or the south? Not so, brothers and friends—please God, ours shall not be so. We will walk on our own feet; we will work with our own hands; we will speak our own minds. The study of letters shall be no longer a name for pity, for doubt, and for sensual indulgence. [107] The dread of man and the love of man shall be a wall of defense and a wreath of joy around all. A nation of men will for the first time exist, because each believes himself inspired by the Divine Soul which also inspires all men.

VI

THAT, then, is what Emerson said, eighty-six years ago. What do we think of it? We know what Brother Pierce thought of it, and what was the verdict of Holmes and Lowell and Carlyle. I have amused myself—though I may have wearied you—by intimating what this hearer and that, among the long-vanished audience, may have surmised or hoped or resolved in his own heart, as those beautiful cadences ceased at last, and the great hour is over. I might tell what was said in the newspapers and in the Reviews, and how the entire edition of the address was sold out in one month, whereas it took thirteen years to sell the first five hundred copies of the orator's book on "Nature." Yet all such evidence, interesting as it may be to one's antiquarian curiosity, does not fully explain the meaning or the power of Emerson's address.

The words of Emerson's speech are still legible upon the printed page, but how small a portion of any speech are the mere words! Boys declaim them in school, "meek young men in libraries" [108] study the sources, literary historians endeavor to reconstruct the time and place of utterance. Yet the magic has fled with the magical hour, and the words seem only the garments of a soul that has escaped. The chemical formula for a great speech seems simple enough, but it is mysterious, like all simple things; it is *a Man plus the atmosphere of a given epoch.* The speech falls flat if it be uttered a year, a month, a day earlier or later than its appointed hour. See young Wendell Phillips fighting his way to the platform of Faneuil Hall on December 8th of that very year, 1837, to defend the memory of Lovejoy from the attack of the Attorney-General of Massachusetts. It is now or never for what Phillips has to say, and Phillips knows it. See him forty-four years later, in Sanders Theater, as the Phi Beta Kappa orator of 1881, defending Russian Nihilism; some of us can remember the tense excitement of the American public in that hour over the question of freedom in Russia. Almost no one in Sanders Theater knew what Phillips was to say. Official Harvard, as always, distrusted him. His flashing eloquence, that noon, was the electric discharge, through him, of forces greater than the orator. If you will read that address of 1881 to-day, you cannot withhold your admiration for the cunning art of the consummate craftsman. The right words [109] are all there in their right places. But the spell is broken; "the image of the God is gone."

Now, it is a part of the genius and the glory of Emerson that his spoken words have the accent of literature. Their specific form is, indeed, shaped by the heat and pressure of an occasion. But their substance is perdurable. His phrases are final phrases. His aim is Truth, and not mere eloquence. He has, indeed, learned the art of rhetoric from Everett and Webster, but he has also learned, by watching them, to distrust rhetoric—to keep it in its place. He would like to win his immediate audience, no doubt, but he is forever saying to himself, as Lincoln said of his debates with Douglas in 1858, "there is bigger game than this." Lincoln's ultimate object was to justify the fundamental principles of free government. Emerson's goal was the Truth that sets men free. His words are literature because the Truth that he perceived could be revealed only through Beauty. The revealing phrase is lovely, and the uncovered face of Truth is lovelier still. As Emerson discourses of Nature and Books and Action, he lays bare his own mind, as an athlete strips himself for the race. Exquisite perception of external beauty, ripened wisdom, high courage —these were the man, and by their perfect expression of the man's qualities Emerson's addresses win their place as [110] literature. We read them to-day as we read Montaigne or Bacon, as something forever alive.

I remarked to a friend the other day that I was trying to imagine what Emerson would say if he had to make his Phi Beta Kappa speech over again in the present hour. "If Emerson were living to-day," was the reply, "he would be a very different Emerson." In one sense, of course, my friend was right. If Emerson had been born seventy-five years later, he would have read Tolstoy and Ibsen, he would have studied under William James, and he would use a somewhat different vocabulary. It is likely that he would have written no Journals. He would have missed the discipline and support of the Lyceum audiences. But he would certainly be giving Lowell Institute lectures, as of old, and writing for the "Atlantic Monthly," and lunching with the Saturday Club. It is certain that he would be making Phi Beta Kappa speeches, and I think we may be allowed to guess what he would say. He would still, I believe, have a message for you and me, a message for our academic communities, and a counsel of perfection for the United States.

To the private person he would announce, with the old serenity: "The sun shines to-day also"—"and, after sunset, Night and her stars." In uttering this gospel of Nature he would use new terms, [111] for his mind would have been fascinated by the new discoveries. But while the illustrations would be novel, he would still assert the universality of Law. He would still say: Books are good, but the living soul is better. "Do not teach me out of Leibnitz and Schelling, and I shall find it all out myself." He would still preach to us the gospel of the will, or, in William James's phrase, "the will to believe." "When you renounce your early visions, then dies the man in you." Be a unit. In this whirring social machinery of the twentieth century, in this over-organized, sentimentalized, and easily stampeded age, possess your own soul. By and by the snowstorm of illusions will cease, and you will be left alone with the moral laws of the universe, you alone and they alone. When that supreme hour comes meet it without fear.

Emerson's message to the academic community would have, I think, a note of yearning. The historic Emerson always wished to be one of us. There was no time in his long career, his biographer says, when he would not gladly have accepted a professorship of rhetoric in any college. If he were of our generation, but still, as of old, outside of our own immediate circle, would he not say: "O you who are cramped in costly buildings, clogged with routine, preoccupied with administrative machinery, [112] how can you see the sun whether it be shining? Where is your free hour for Night and her stars? You are learned in bibliographies, expert in card catalogues, masters of a thousand specialties. You are documented, certificated, sophisticated. But have you the old eager reverence for the great books? And where, by the way, are your own books? From these thousands of American colleges and universities, how many vital, creative books are born? The university of Walden Pond had 'Whim' written above its doorposts, but it bred literature. There was once a type of productive scholar who may be described as 'he that scattereth, and yet increaseth,' but your amazing and multifarious activity, is not much of it wastage rather than growth? Simplify! Coördinate! Find yourselves, and then lift up your hearts!"

And finally I am sure that the spirit of Emerson, if he were revisiting this "great sensual avaricious America," as the historic Emerson once called it, would have a message for the United States in this hour of cowardice, disillusionment, and inhibition. Unless Emerson came back from the under-world with a changed soul, he would assert the supremacy of moral obligations. He would perceive, as in his lifetime, that a "diffidence in the soul was creeping over the American mind." But he would shame that diffidence. He would [113] rally the distrustful. Can we not hear once more his clear and quiet voice: The gods are forever in their places: first, Righteousness, Justice, and Liberty, and after these, Fellowship and Peace. The Law holds. The foundations of human society are moral foundations. They cannot be shaken, even though whole empires should lose their senses and debauch their souls and go toppling down. Be steady. "This time, like all times, is a very good one, if we but know what to do with it." Behold the Law: "God is, not was; He speaketh, not spake." The world is very wide, very strange, it terrifies us, it seems plunging from its orbit. But it cannot plunge from its orbit; that was fixed before the foundation of the world. Patience—patience. Our earth is whirling on its way from God and to God, and the law of its being is the same law of obedience and of faith which is written in the heart of the obscurest scholar.

QUESTIONS FOR DISCUSSION

Understanding the Text

1. This informal literary essay attempts to recreate the scene and atmosphere of Emerson's speech. What narrative devices and characteristics of style does the author employ to give the reader a sense of being present for the occasion? How would you describe the tone, or attitude toward the reader? Do the style and tone contribute to your interest in the essay or detract from it? Explain.

2. Addressed to an educated audience, Perry's essay mentions many people renowned in America's cultural history. Who are the following people, and what are they famous for? William Dean Howells, George Ripley, William Cullen Bryant, Daniel Webster, Andrews Norton, Richard Henry Dana, James Russell Lowell, Wendell Phillips, Edward Everett Hale, Edward Everett, Oliver Wendell Holmes, William Ellery Channing.

3. Perry says that Emerson, like Anne Hutchinson, was a "champion of rebellion." What were their rebellions about, and in what way were they similar or dissimilar?

4. What was the "unhappy division of the Congregational churches which had absorbed so much of the attention of New England for thirty years"? Who were the "Liberals" and the "Orthodox" in that division, and what did they stand for?

5. Dr. John Pierce appears as an onlooker who clings to the views of the conservative past. How is the generation gap illustrated by Pierce's presence in the essay? What tone does Perry take toward Pierce? Why does he refer to Pierce so many times and in so many places in the essay?

6. What are the characteristics in Emerson's speech which so excited Holmes, Lowell, and Carlyle? Can you isolate the passages that contain the inspiration which they speak of? Analyze the style as well as the thought of these passages.

7. Perry notes that some of the college Overseers were probably absent because Emerson was an unknown, small-town preacher and unsuccessful author—"only a stick-it minister from Concord, author of an anonymous, unintelligible, and unsold little book on 'Nature.'" Explain the irony of this statement. What other examples of irony do you find in Perry's essay?

54

Evaluating Ideas

1. Briefly evaluate Perry's essay, commenting especially on the extent to which it aided your understanding or appreciation of Emerson's speech.

2. From Perry's summary of earlier Phi Beta Kappa addresses, it is clear that the speakers frequently discussed the "duties and responsibilities" of the American scholar in a developing republic. Is this topic a meaningful one today? If so, what are these duties and responsibilities?

3. In alluding to William Ellery Channing's famous essay on "National Literature" (1831), Perry notes the Unitarian minister's prediction that in America power will pass increasingly, not into the hands of government, but into the hands of "those who think and write." What does Emerson's essay say about the future power of the American scholar who, like Emerson himself, was often a man who thought and wrote? Has Channing's prediction been realized? Explain. What is the situation today of the scholar who "thinks and writes" in relation to the power of government?

4. Perry's reference to Emerson's poet-friend Jones Very as a "half-crazed, half-inspired tutor of Greek" introduces an idea common in romantic thought and literature —that earth's madness is heaven's sense, that society sometimes takes spiritual wisdom or inspiration to be insanity. Jones Very spent some time in the Charlestown insane asylum in 1838, although some of his friends, including Emerson, were suspicious that he was saner than the society that committed him. Very believed that he had previously died on earth and was now a spiritual entity. In 1838 Emerson said of Very: "I wish the whole world were as mad as he." Perry quotes the remark made to Carlyle by the English writer Harriet Martineau about Emerson's own thought: "Some say it is inspired, some say it is mad." What thoughts in "The American Scholar" would be most likely to raise the question of inspiration or madness? Name some of the inspired men or women of the past who have been treated as mad. What prophetic voices in America today are, in your opinion, saner than the society that suspects them of madness?

5. Perry suggests that if Emerson were to make his speech "over again in the present hour," it would be a somewhat different speech. Which parts of the speech do you think he would retain today? Which have become less meaningful because of the changes made by history?

6. Does Perry's reconstruction of what Emerson would have said in the 1920's seem relevant to the individual and the academic community today? For example, are you becoming "documented, certificated, sophisticated" but without that creative spirit and "old eager reverence" for great books which Emerson's scholar exhibited?

If you are moved by important books, what books are they? In what ways are they "great books"?

7. In somewhat rapturous terms, Perry remarks that Emerson's essay is literature "because the Truth that he perceived could be revealed only through Beauty" and because Emerson, in revealing himself in the essay, combined perception of beauty, mature wisdom, and courage. These were the characteristics of Emerson, says Perry, "and by their perfect expression of the man's qualities Emerson's addresses win their place as literature." Some modern students, and teachers as well, challenge such praise of Emerson and think his essays inappropriate for introductory college courses because in style and content they are thought to be, among other things, bland, sententious, preachy, obscure, rambling, impractical. Give your own response to Perry's comment. In what respects is "The American Scholar" an appropriate or inappropriate essay for classroom use today?

THE AMERICAN SCHOLAR

John Erskine

John Erskine was a music and literary critic and a popular novelist. As a teacher at Columbia and platform lecturer he was noted for his wit and learning.

[5] IN 1834 Emerson read the Poem at the annual meeting of the Phi Beta Kappa Society of Harvard College. On August 31, 1837, he read before the same body the famous address on "The American Scholar." James Russell Lowell, recalling the occasion thirty years later, said it "was an event without any former parallel in our literary annals, a scene to be always treasured in the memory for its picturesqueness and its inspiration. What crowded and breathless aisles, what windows clustering with eager heads, what enthusiasm of approval, what grim silence of foregone dissent!" Oliver Wendell Holmes called the address "our intellectual Declaration of Independence. . . . It was easy to find fault with an expression here and there. The dignity, not to say the formality, of an academic assembly, was startled by the realism that looked for the infinite in 'the meal in the firkin; the milk in the pan.' They could understand the deep thoughts suggested by 'the meanest flower that blows,' but these domestic illustrations had a kind of nursery homeliness about them which the grave professors and sedate clergymen were unused to expect on so stately an occasion. But the young men went out from it as if a prophet had been proclaiming to them, 'Thus saith the Lord.' No listener ever forgot that address, and among all the noble utterances of the speaker it may be questioned if one ever contained more truth in language more like that of genuine inspiration."

Those listeners who crowded the hall with their enthusiasm or with their grim dissent, heard these words:

From *The American Scholar*, I (Winter, 1932), 5–15. Reprinted by permission.

[Several pages of direct quotation from Emerson's address are omitted here. They include Emerson's definition of the scholar, his description of the influences of books and action, and his comments on the scholar's functions.]

[10] This is the doctrine which those excited listeners disagreed with or approved. Part of it has often been repeated during the ninety-five years since Emerson spoke. We have often been told that American art is less creative than it should be, that our scholarship is timid, that we lean too much upon the tradition of the Old World. It is often the European now who points out this fault of ours, but many Americans also are concerned about it.

Less often we are reminded of the positive note in Emerson's address, that the moment we live in is the best moment for us, and that it lies in our power, as much as it ever lay in the power of our fathers, to enjoy an original relation with the universe.

Emerson might have said that the weakness which he was describing in American scholarship besets scholarship everywhere. By his very nature the scholar loves the past and reveres the accomplishments of his predecessors. Only too easily his most creditable piety passes over into formula or inertia, and his spiritual aspirations which ought to lean toward the future relapse into a meticulous nostalgia. This was true of many scholars in the stirring time of Elizabeth, in the very mid-pulse of the Renaissance. The Gabriel Harveys at whom Shakespeare and his fellow dramatists liked to poke fun were noble scholars, but they were scholars.

If Emerson made his criticism exclusively of his own land, it was because he wished to attend strictly to what is our own business, it was because he wished to provide in advance no excuse for us, it was because in his philosophy each one of us naturally represents the whole race, and should assume the human responsibility in his own person. Perhaps also it was because he felt, as many others have believed, that the situation of the American scholar in history lays upon him peculiar obligations and provides him with unique opportunities. His country must be built up quickly. Its culture must be developed in only a fraction of the time through which European culture slowly grew. But on the other hand this evolution is to be pushed by men and women who bring with them when they arrive on these shores a mature civilization, and who therefore are spared the infinite number of steps by which most people have climbed from a primitive barbarousness to an elaborate and spiritual society. If the Continent is to be filled up so quickly and its resources exploited almost overnight by an influx of peoples already educated in civilization, then [11] the result in our intellectual life ought to be something new, a more than usual vigorous attack on the problems in front of us, a clearer sight of things as they are, a sharper decision between better and worse, between good and evil.

In this present year of grace, and in this first number of the Phi Beta Kappa Quarterly, which has assumed for its name the title of Emerson's address, it is inevitable that the American Scholar should take an inventory of himself to see whether he is after all these years yet standing on his own feet, yet solving his own problems rather than the problems of men long dead, whether he yet has learned that the moment in which he lives is for him the richest moment. No doubt each scholar will respond to this scrutiny with his own personal faith. If the progress of American scholarship is measured in the sciences, we can make Emerson a good answer, though I fancy we should have to go outside of academic circles for some of our best illustrations. Emerson would have drawn deep satisfaction from the contributions of Thomas Edison to our civilization, and perhaps an equal satisfaction from the significance, social and otherwise, of Henry Ford's car. Such contributions would seem to him proper to America. He would be no doubt happy in the airship which the Wright brothers developed and which America at first left to other lands to appreciate. He would think it a happy sign of our sanity that this country has made vast strides in the development of the telephone, the radio, the films, and in the more remote and less obvious regions of science; in medicine, in chemistry, in physics. He would no doubt find cause to give thanks that the American scholar does his part.

But Emerson used the word scholar in the somewhat limited and homely sense of the book man, the historian, the critic, the linguist, the philosopher. And speaking in a great college he addressed his famous warning to those of us who are entrusted with the education of youth. What would he think of us if the address were now to be made again?

If he were available we should of course invite him to make an address. Phi Beta Kappa orations are more numerous than they used to be, and the local committee must expend some energy in order to secure a speaker who will draw. Emerson undoubtedly would be among the available. If he came to us in the beginning of June, not [12] in the end of August, he would very probably notice the building operations which our campus would be undertaking. A benefactor, doubtless, would have left us money for a building for which to carry on some phase of American scholarship. No doubt the building would be designed by an excellent architect, and at their best, American architects are superb. But if the building had already started to rise, Emerson would notice that its architecture was not American. At one or two colleges it might be, but in the majority it would be Gothic—a peculiar literary kind of Gothic— or it would suggest the Italian Renaissance, or Greece, or Rome.

It is at first hard to see why the American colleges have been so steadily abandoning the lovely architecture with which many of them began, and putting on instead the Gothic garment. One by one the college chapels of the founders become Medieval cathedrals. No one charges that the college is changing its religion or that the Gothic chancel with its place for the high altar means anything to the student body, theologically speaking, which the battered old oak desk did not express, but here in our astonishing landscape rise the vaulted roofs, the clerestories, the windows of colored glass, the mysterious shadows and symbols of another age.

And the Gothic garment is put on for the library too, for the dining hall, even for the dormitories. In an age when the manufacture of glass is no mystery we revert for piety's sake to small and insufficient windows, and live in gloom, helped out by electric bulbs. Moreover, it is the great honor of many of our colleges that they were established not in the Medieval way by the individual patron, but by the will of the community, demanding that its sons and daughters should be taught. But since it is hard to think of a community as a dramatic figure, the colleges which enjoyed this democratic origin tend more and more to invent a myth about some individual and make him a founder. One good college song can upset history. The boys at Amherst sing of Lord Jeffrey, who went to his grave, poor man, without having heard of them or their college, whereas the magnificent farmers who made the college possible are quite forgotten. Why should American college boys prefer to give their own traditions this twist away from the democratic toward what ought to seem to them futile and patronizing? I think the reason is that the human animal likes to make his environment accord with the preoccupation [13] of his thoughts. If we are an engineer, or a musician, or a hunter, the room which we live in will sooner or later illustrate in some way our profession. It is an economy of spirit to permit no contrast between what we see inside of us and what we must look upon outside. If our colleges are slowly taking on a Medieval exterior, it is, I believe, because the academic life is still Medieval. It apes unconsciously or intentionally the manners of older lands, and it addresses itself far more than we like to admit to the solution of other men's problems which no longer concern us. The evil is not that we are minding other folks' business—it is that we include our own. We have had enough economic theory in the United States to sink a ship—and behold the ship is sunk!

It is easy to name the Medieval aspects of American scholarship which show themselves in the social organization of our colleges. We have dormitories and cloisters, and certain rules tending toward chaperonage. This is all an inheritance from the monastic ideal. Because the monasteries are still strong in our thoughts, we assume that boys and girls should not marry while they are studying, matrimony and the pursuit of truth being incompatible. In some colleges still a student would fail to get his degree if he married in his junior or senior year. This monastic tradition disguises itself in the press of college life, and in the fetish of a certain kind of college spirit which if carried to a conclusion would make the American college a true monastery or nunnery, a place where the boys or the girls would be separated from the rest of the world, each sex for a time forgetting its relation to general society, and meditating exclusively on higher things.

The monastery would be a possible ideal if we followed it completely. When we segregate boys from general society, we ought to feed their minds with ideas which do not derive from worldly sources. As a matter of fact, these unfortunate youngsters who must be in the dormitory at certain hours, entertain girls only at certain times, and re-visit the normal life only at week ends, are asked to read in class "Romeo and Juliet," or the poetry of Walt Whitman, or the novels of Dickens and Thackeray, or Meredith or Hardy— intellectual fare never designed for monasteries, all exciting the readers' curiosity for the great world. In our colleges, in spite of the Medieval grip on them, the youngsters bootleg life. They would rather not [14] bootleg it, they would rather be taught to study it frankly, and they would rather study their own life with its immediate problems than what seemed a problem to Shakespeare or some other writer of a far country or a distant time. The American scholars guide our youth so that the young people do not know what their own problems are. This is probably true, but their teachers ought to know; at

least the teachers ought to be aware of *their* own problems even if they cannot imagine the problems of their charges.

There is no doubt at all what Emerson would be thinking of those courses
of philosophy which still clutter our catalogs, in which you are taught the solution of subtle problems, the existence of which you did not know until you
took the course. The philosopher's contribution to truth when you first hear it
seems silly or meaningless, but he assures you that the significance will be
clear when you have learned the problem, and you take the course in search
for the question which the silly answer will dispose of. When philosophy,
however, has been great, it has not made up its problems, it has rather addressed itself to the problems of the age. In our day we face immense questions in ethics, both personal and communal, in the organization of society, of
business, of the home. We must give a new account of the arts and their relation to the education and the daily life of average men and women. We are
redefining the scope and the period of education, and we are uncertain about
the future of organized religion. These and other problems immediate with us
the American scholar ought logically to handle. Too often the problems of
men die with them, and the problem which is only temporary deserves to die.
What could be less lucky for scholarship than that it should continue to pon-
der the question which had not vitality enough to repeat itself?

In his address Emerson took care to guard against the charge that he saw
no value at all in the past, but in all his writings he liked to make the cardi-
nal distinction between the things which have a certain order in time and the
things which are timeless. Out of the centuries come a few men, a few occasions, a few ideas, a few problems which seem to belong to all time. Once
they have sifted themselves from the irrelevant things of their own age, they
need no chronology, they are all up-to-date, and are of one date. When Emerson had occasion to name some of his heroes, he liked to jumble the centuries,
putting Washington, perhaps, before Caesar, or Napoleon before [15] Alexan-
der. This apparent confusion he made by design as though to liberate the
mind from too exclusive preoccupation with the calendar. He liked every illustration he could find in American life of this freedom of the past which
some of our critics have called irreverence. Doubtless he enjoyed that passage
in "Snow Bound" in which the young Dartmouth student recites to the delight
of the farmer's household stories of Greek mythology in modern terms, making the gods and goddesses seem as though they were neighbors in the berry

patch. This transfer of all human experience into what we can understand in our own immediate faith was for Emerson the secret of contact with the universe. We were to find the Over-soul by that supreme exercise of the imagination which enables a man to see himself.

Translated into the plainest terms Emerson's doctrine means for us that American scholarship at this moment ought to attack directly and with no embarrassment of tradition the questions of our life in this year and this month, throwing the past, as one might think, bodily, and starting fresh as though we were the first to use the mind. The best of the past would still be with us, absorbed in our being and in our unconscious culture, yet if it is not yet so absorbed we had better discard it, since after so much worship of it it is an irrelevant covering, an exotic garment, like the Medieval towers we insist on raising among our maples and elms and pines.

QUESTIONS FOR DISCUSSION

Understanding the Text

1. John Erskine's essay was written in 1932, during the dark days of the depression which began in 1929. In what ways does the essay reveal the time of its composition? Why does Erskine hold his generation of American scholars partly responsible for America's economic and social failure? In what ways had they failed to follow Emerson's advice? In what ways had they been successful?

2. What is the significance of Erskine's attack on the architecture of American colleges? What does the fondness for medieval design reveal about the American scholar and the academic community? What did Emerson say about a nation which "apes unconsciously or intentionally the manners of older lands"? What are the chief characteristics of the architecture of your own college? What do they reveal about its history or educational philosophy?

3. The first part of Erskine's essay is mainly a summary or reduction of the material in "The American Scholar." Is there value for students in this kind of reduction or would additional study of Emerson's own text be more rewarding? Explain what is gained or lost by the study of Erskine's summary of the essay's content. The second part of Erskine's essay applies Emerson's address to the 1930's. Does this process contribute to your understanding of Emerson, or do the author's comments about his own decade seem meaningless or irrelevant to students of the 1970's? Support your answer.

Evaluating Ideas

1. Erskine says that in Emerson's philosophy "each one of us naturally represents the whole race, and should assume the human responsibility in his own person." What evidence do you find in "The American Scholar" to support Erskine's statement? In your view, do individuals represent humanity, or is this just romantic idealism? What "human responsibility" does the individual have toward the race?

2. In his comments on the monastic tradition in college life, Erskine says that students are sometimes "separated from the rest of the world, each sex for a time forgetting its relation to general society, and meditating exclusively on higher

things." Does this situation still prevail in American colleges and universities? Explain. To what extent are you required to "bootleg life" into your own institution?

3. Erskine complains that the American scholars who are also teachers "guide our youth so that the young people do not know what their own problems are." Is this criticism relevant today? Or is it more accurate to say that students know what their problems are, but some teachers and administrators do not? What are some specific examples of this situation?

4. Speculating on what Emerson would think of twentieth-century America, Erskine says that "Emerson would have drawn deep satisfaction from the contributions of Thomas Edison to our civilization, and perhaps an equal satisfaction from the significance, social and otherwise, of Henry Ford's car." What were the major contributions of Edison? Explain the social significance of the Ford automobile in our society. What evidence is there in "The American Scholar" that Emerson would approve or disapprove the social influences of the automobile?

5. Erskine declares that many colleges with simple democratic origins feel it necessary to invent myths about their founders or their historical past because "the human animal likes to make his environment accord with the preoccupation of his thoughts." What are some of the common myths with which colleges and universities like to embellish their traditions? What myths are part of your own school's tradition? (If your instructor regularly attends academic events such as founders' day ceremonies and commencement exercises, he may be persuaded to contribute to your answer.)

6. Erskine contends that college catalogs are cluttered with philosophy courses "in which you are taught the solution of subtle problems, the existence of which you did not know until you took the course." Is this a fair criticism of the curriculum today? Explain. What is your response to his view that when philosophy "has been great, it has not made up its problems, it has rather addressed itself to the problems of the age"? In "The American Scholar" does Emerson deal mainly with "the problems of the age," or with timeless philosophical problems, or with both? Explain.

7. Erskine concludes that we should follow Emerson's doctrine and attack directly the questions of our own time, "throwing the past, as one might think, bodily, and starting fresh as though we were the first to use the mind." Do you agree with this tendency to disregard the past? It is sometimes said that this generation of college students thinks that "history began in 1945." What is your response to this criticism? What does Emerson say in his essay about the uses of history? Do you agree with him? In 1839 Emerson made the following entry in his journal:

> There is no history. There is only biography. The attempt to perpetuate, to
> fix a thought or principle, fails continually. You can only live for yourself;

your action is good only whilst it is alive,—whilst it is in you. The awkward imitation of it by your child or your disciple is not a repetition of it, is not the same thing, but another thing. The new individual must work out the whole problem of science, letters and theology for himself; can owe his fathers nothing. There is no history; only biography.

Is the sense of this passage expressed also in "The American Scholar"? Explain. What is your own response to the journal entry?

THE AMERICAN SCHOLAR TODAY

Henry Nash Smith

Henry Nash Smith is a literary scholar and professor of English at the
University of California, Berkeley. His well-known book called *Virgin Land*
(1950) gives a comprehensive view of the myths and symbols in our inter-
pretation of the American West.

[191] IN HISTORIES of literature Ralph Waldo Emerson's address, "The
American Scholar," delivered before the Phi Beta Kappa Society at Harvard
in August, 1837, is noted as a second declaration of American independence
from Europe—a declaration of literary and cultural independence. The ring-
ing phrases in which he announces the new era of freedom for the American
writer are among the best known in our literature: "Our day of dependence,
our long apprenticeship to the learning of other lands, draws to a close." Or
again: "We have listened too long to the courtly muses of Europe." The ad-
monition and the prophecy were true and timely in the 1830's. But they sound
almost prehistoric in a day when French novelists try to write like Faulkner
and not only Hemingway but even Salinger is a household word in Britain. In
any case, literary nationalism is only an incidental topic for Emerson. The
sentences I have quoted come from the introduction and the conclusion of the
address. In between, he hardly mentions the theme.

What he is primarily concerned with is how the young American scholar
can find a place in American society. Despite the note of urgency in the address, or perhaps because of it, Emerson's argument is remarkably obscure.
He is using the term Scholar in a special and unusual sense. As he says, the
subject was prescribed by usage: an address with this title was delivered

From *Southwest Review*, XLVIII (Summer, 1963), 191–199. Copyright © 1963 by South-
ern Methodist University Press and reprinted by permission of the author and the publisher.

every year. Then, as now, the phrase usually designated those among the students of the college who had distinguished themselves by excellence in their studies. But Emerson takes it in a quite different sense. He is really talking about a group of young men—in which he includes himself—whose love of letters and of ideas places them in a "state of virtual hostility to society." From a conventional standpoint Emerson's arbitrary redefinition of a prescribed subject was indecorous—only a little less outrageous than his performance the following year, when he agreed to make the commencement address for the Harvard Divinity School and blandly informed his audience that historical Christianity was dead. A leading professor in the school published a pamphlet denouncing that address as "the latest form of infidelity," and Emerson was not invited back to Harvard for some thirty years.

"The American Scholar" is not so obviously subversive, but its implications amount to a kind of polite anarchy. Although Emerson's tone is austere, his [192] point of view is remarkably close to that of the Beat writers of our own day. It is no doubt grotesque to conjure up an image of Emerson in sandals and beard beating on bongo drums, but the suggestion may seem less preposterous if you think of Whitman as Emerson's most faithful disciple in the next generation, and then go on from Whitman to Hart Crane and Henry Miller and Jack Kerouac.

Emerson had made a false start in life by entering the profession that was traditional in his family—the ministry—and despite a considerable degree of success had discovered when he was twenty-nine years old that he simply could not go on. I do not know how to convey his state of mind except by using clichés: he was alienated from the value system of Brahmin Boston. He did not know what to do with himself; he could not accept any of the ways of life or careers offered to him by the world he lived in. By 1837 he had spent five years of intense self-scrutiny trying to discover a role he could accept without doing violence to his own nature. His efforts to deal with his personal problem had taken two principal forms. Since he was by training a theologian and philosopher, he had seized upon certain abstract ideas, such as his notion of self-reliance and his special cult of Nature, in order to provide for himself a body of doctrine to replace the faith of the Unitarian church he had left. But he was also an artist; and along with this abstract, speculative attack on his problem he had dealt with it imaginatively by devising a series of more or less shadowy, half-realized allegorical figures to which he had given names such as the Student, the Seer, the Transcendentalist, the Poet, the Idealist—all of them representing efforts to conceive of an ideal character and ideal functions that he could adopt as a guide to his own life. Emerson now adds the Scholar to the list of these figures that express his estrangement from existing institutions. The address is obscure because he has not yet solved his personal problem of vocation and thus cannot bring into focus the image to which he applies the name of the American Scholar.

In various essays of this period Emerson tries to show what these young men with knives in their brains—as he calls them—objected to in the world about them. Their adversaries include "the sturdy capitalist" who builds a cubical banking-house, laying its foundation "deep and square on blocks of Quincy granite." Or again the enemy is "brokers, attorneys, and congressmen." The Transcendentalists, he says, "withdraw themselves from the common labors and competitions of the market and the caucus." "What you call your fundamental institutions," he goes on, "your great and holy causes, seem to them great abuses, and, when nearly seen, paltry matters." In a word, the Idealists "are not good citizens, not good members of society . . ." "State Street," he added in a later essay, "had an instinct that they invalidated contracts and threatened the stability of stocks; and it did not fancy brusque manners."

A number of books widely read in recent years have described mid-twentieth-century American society from a point of view closely resembling that of Emerson's [193] Scholar or Transcendentalist looking at Massachusetts in the 1830's. Some of these books, like C. Wright Mills's *White Collar* or William H. Whyte, Jr.'s *The Organization Man*, include a good deal of empirical data drawn from formal surveys and statistical tables. Others are more personal and hortatory. But they all say in effect that the rudimentary commercial interests which Emerson identified with State Street and Quincy capitalists have developed in the twentieth century into the imposing and apparently monolithic structure of modern American business. Another recent critic, Paul Goodman, says that the "organized system of production and sales and its culture" which dominates American life seems completely sterile to large numbers of young men reaching maturity. He maintains that most of the jobs created by the system are unnecessary, and that "a young fellow looking for a manly occupation" is in a worse plight now than ever before.

It's hard to grow up [he writes] when there isn't enough man's work. There is "nearly full employment" (with highly significant exceptions), but there get to be fewer jobs that are necessary or unquestionably useful; that require energy and draw on some of one's best capacities; and that can be done keeping one's honor and dignity.

The title of Mr. Goodman's book is *Growing Up Absurd*. This might well stand also as a title for the address on "The American Scholar." Where Emerson declares that the Scholar and the Transcendentalist "feel the disproportion between their faculties and the work offered them," that "they are striking work, and crying out for somewhat worthy to do!" Goodman reports that "the disaffected youth who are articulate . . .—for instance, the Beat or Angry young men" have for their main topic "the 'system' with which they refuse to cooperate." The Beat and the Angry young men are a small minority, a kind of elite, among the various groups described by Mr. Goodman. Coming usually (like Emerson's Scholar) from middle-class families and having a good deal of formal education, they can make themselves heard, in contrast with the much greater number of lower-class youths who have no channel of expression except outright delinquency. Even in the middle class, the young men who acknowledge their disaffection and accept the consequences of it are statistically insignificant beside the vast majority who pass with a minimum of reflection into the places open to them in the job market. But as Mr. Goodman insists, it is the articulate few who make us aware of the price that is paid by the conformist many. He emphasizes the plight of the so-called junior executive, a few years out of college, who works in some nontechnical capacity for a large corporation. Such a man, says Mr. Goodman, is caught in

a terrible contradiction. He is cynical about the aims of the firm, yet he fears his own ineptitude will be found out. He has no recourse to concrete performance, for there is little contact with unambiguous material and there are no objective standards. How to meet a purely subjective demand? . . . he has to get by by role playing, interpersonal relations abstracted from both animal desire or tangible achievement. He meets expectations, he conforms, he one-ups, he proves he must know how by attaining a higher status.

[194] In Emerson's language this had come out as follows: the disaffected Scholars and Transcendentalists

have made the experiment, and found that from the liberal professions to the coarsest manual labor, and from the courtesies of the academy and the college to the conventions of the cotillon-room and the morning call, there is a spirit of cowardly compromise and seeming, which intimates a frightful scepticism, a life without love, and an activity without an aim.

The Organization Man complements *Growing Up Absurd*. Whereas Mr. Goodman devotes most of his space to various kinds of rebelliousness, Mr. Whyte focusses on the "acquiescence" and political apathy of college seniors about to enter business. His main topic, in other words, is what Emerson calls "cowardly compromise and seeming" and Mr. Goodman calls "hipster skepticism." Mr. Whyte's book was published in 1956, and therefore deals with a state of affairs now almost a decade in the past. But I do not think it is out of date. We have heard a good deal lately about a supposed wave of radicalism among college students. For example, there is the film called *Operation Abolition* that purports to reveal Communist infiltration of the student bodies of California universities. In my opinion the motion of dangerous radicalism in American universities is of a piece with most current excitement over subversive conspiracies within the United States—that is, a pure, or rather an impure, fabrication for political ends. I happen to know that *Operation Abolition* juggles and fabricates evidence to support its thesis, and I suspect that other charges of this nature warrant Mr. Whyte's comment that ". . . whenever a poll indicates that students don't realize that business makes only about 6 per cent profit, there is a flurry of demands for some new crusade to rescue our youth from socialist tendencies."

My own impressions support Mr. Whyte's contention that young men finishing college are already for the most part under the influence of the business system. He begins a chapter called "A Generation of Bureaucrats" by describing a visit to the placement center at Purdue University where recruiters for business concerns were interviewing applicants for jobs. He was impressed by the quiet efficiency of the operation, the standardized procedures, the atmosphere of managerial calm in which, as he says, "scores of young men were, every hour on the hour, making the decisions that would determine their whole future life." And interviews with graduating seniors convinced him that most of them accepted with little or no question what might be called the corporation ethos. "The lawyers, the doctors, the scientists," he says, "are also subject to the same centralization, the same trend to group work and to bureaucratization." The students he talked with were "above all, conservative"—not in the sense that their ideas belong within the "historic sweep" of conservative thought, but in the sense that they accept the status quo without any inclination to question methods or results.

The organization mentality becomes almost compulsory in a society that has made a major industry of compiling personnel records. The college student of [195] today knows that every friendship he forms, every meeting he attends, every trip he makes is liable to be recorded somewhere in the files of a government agency or to be made the subject of later scrutiny. Even what he says in class discussion or in papers submitted in courses may be inquired into by the ubiquitous investigators when he applies for a job or enters military service. Only a hero or a saint could be indifferent to the pressures toward conformity that bear upon these youngsters now almost from childhood. One of the most melancholy experiences I have ever had is to observe police photographers taking candid camera shots of students standing on the sidewalk listening to a speech in favor of disarmament.

Although Emerson's world seems almost prelapsarian in its immunity from the investigative techniques of modern governments and corporations, in its main outlines his indictment of American society is remarkably similar to that of twentieth-century critics. They are all, no doubt, hyperbolical in their language. Emerson sometimes adopts the manner of the jeremiads launched from the pulpit by a long line of New England clergymen, and Mr. Goodman's book, in particular, is an act of prophecy rather than a scientific treatise. Nevertheless, these critics are dealing with a real issue: the tendency of economic forces in American society to create an overrigid institutional structure in which basic needs of human beings are sacrificed to the drive for profits. Both in the 1830's and in the 1960's sensitive and articulate observers have put themselves on record as finding the system on the whole unattractive. They have exhorted young men not yet hopelessly committed to what Emerson calls the Establishment to reject the goals and the values which it would impose on them.

I have pointed out that Emerson's ideal figure of the scholar presents this criticism in imaginative terms. But Emerson's gift as an artist was lyrical; he had none of the novelist's ability to project characters dramatically and involve them in significant actions. As a result, the long series of hero types that appear in his journals and public addresses during the decade after his withdrawal from the ministry is a company of spectral abstractions, of ghosts. Other nineteenth-century American writers with greater powers of dramatization added more fully realized characters to this company of Outsiders. Hawthorne's Hester Prynne is the most vivid example, but the list would have to include such widely various creations as Melville's Ahab and Ishmael and Bartleby, the persona who speaks in Emily Dickinson's poems, Christopher Newman and Lambert Strether and many other characters in Henry James, and the remarkable series of what have been called Transcendent Figures in the later work of Mark Twain.

Although this random inventory shows that the figure of the Outsider can be used to great effect in fiction, he can never be a hero in the usual sense of the word because he is by definition at odds with society. As Sean O'Faolain says in his book on *The Vanishing Hero* (1956), "the Hero . . . is a purely social creation. He represents, that is to say, a socially approved norm, for representing which to [196] the satisfaction of society he is decorated with a title." The conceptual hero has in our times been replaced "by what, for want of a better word, we have . . . come to call the anti-Hero." He is not a social creation. He is his own creation, that is, the author's personal creation. He is "a much less tidy and comfortable concept since . . . he is always represented as groping, puzzled, cross, mocking, frustrated, isolated in his manful or blundering attempts to establish his own personal, suprasocial codes." Whatever he is, "weak or brave, brainy or bewildered," his one abiding characteristic is that, like his author-creator, he is never able to see any pattern in life and rarely its destination.

Mr. O'Faolain is discussing a trend in European literature. But I think you will agree with me that Emerson's Scholar is a literary ancestor of Mr. O'Faolain's anti-Hero, and that American literature during the past hundred years has been specially prolific in characters belonging to this category. Nowadays serious American fiction seems almost exclusively populated by anti-heroes. In a pretentious but useful survey of the contemporary American novel published in 1961 under the title *Radical Innocence*, Ihab Hassan of Wesleyan College maintains that our writers almost without exception believe that "the contemporary world presents a continued affront to man, and that his response must therefore be the response of the rebel or victim . . ." It is true that the nightmare quality of the work of the Norman Mailers, the William Styrons, the Bernard Malamuds, the Ralph Ellisons owes something to the sheer propagation of literary conventions, a modern Gothicism. I am not proposing their books as reliable documentary guides to American life in the 1960's. But they have a value as undocumentary guides. They are an index to states of mind which the novelists magnify by several diameters and throw on the screen in monstrous technicolor enlargements; but the states of mind are real. The spectacular vices and deformities, physical and spiritual, of the protagonists in recent fiction are a kind of code used to give emphasis to an all-out attack on the merely conformist virtues and the outward neatness and efficiency of a society that is inwardly empty. Accurately deciphered, the code conveys along with much nonsense an impressive vote of no confidence in the dominant goals and methods of our civilization.

The virtual unanimity of the verdict of our serious novelists—by which I mean those who are trying to tell the truth about contemporary experience—stands out clearly if we compare their work with popular or middlebrow fiction. My information on this topic is not absolutely up to date, but I made a study several years ago of all American novels published between 1948 and 1957 which had sold more than a million copies. The titles on the list are familiar. It included such masterpieces as *Marjorie Morningstar, The Man in the Gray Flannel Suit, Not as a Stranger,* and *Peyton Place.* These novels, and most of the others I examined, are concerned with the same general topic that is almost obsessive in serious fiction: the relation of the individual to society. But the authors of bestsellers adopt exactly the opposite attitude from the serious writers. Their basic plot [197] deals with a protagonist somehow at odds with the community. This distressing state of affairs can go on for a long time, because in that decade best-sellers often ran to seven or eight hundred pages. But in the end the rebellious or mixed-up or arrogant or perhaps merely individualistic protagonist recognizes that the community was right all along, and comes back into the fold of conformity.

The serious novels of recent years are of course more various than the best-sellers, but none of them restores the protagonist to real harmony with society. Sometimes, like Ellison's Invisible Man, he makes a desperate effort to establish contact with his fellow human beings, but meeting only chaos and hostility, withdraws into the isolation of an actual or symbolic underground hiding-place. Even a writer with Saul Bellow's power of comic affirmation can do no more than leave his protagonist Augie March in a state of suspense, still uncommitted, involved in shady deals on the black market, and merely ready for whatever may turn up next. A more characteristic ending for the career of an anti-hero is perhaps the decision of William Styron's erratic, driven painter Cass Kinsolving to settle down into a life of outward conformity as a cartoonist, but with complete indifference toward the beliefs and values of the community. The extraordinary tenuousness of whatever affirmation may be involved in such a decision is evident in Kinsolving's explanation that although he had found no belief to support him, he chose being rather than nothingness because "to choose between them was simply to choose being, not for the sake of being, or even the love of being, much less the desire to be forever—but in the hope of being what I could be for a time." A variant form of this acted-out irony is presented in Walker Percy's *The Movie-Goer*, where the protagonist goes through the routine of a stockbroker's office but places his humdrum everyday world and the blatantly unreal world of the films to which he is addicted on exactly the same plane of neither being nor nonbeing, neither illusion nor actuality.

Acceptance of an imposed role, an absolute divorce between the inner and the outer life, the oversophisticated irony of pretending to be a square while actually being "beat": these are the symptoms by which literature reveals a society that has lost its sense of meaning and purpose. Believing that he faced a situation of this sort in New England in the 1830's, Emerson tried valiantly to discover a way out for the disaffected Scholar-Transcendentalist. Sometimes he seems to think there is no solution for the problem: the Scholar is moral man existing alone in a vacuum of values, with nothing to go on except his own consciousness or, in the Transcendental vocabulary, his intuitions. There is undoubtedly a strain of existentialism in Emerson. At the other extreme, he also fell back intermittently on an archaic kind of supernaturalism, maintaining (perhaps in desperation) that the Scholar had a messianic mission, that he could "descend a redeemer into Nature," bringing health and salvation to mankind by miraculous means. Yet in between these limits of near-despair and megalomania, Emerson proposes a technique of survival for the Scholar that [198] will bear the test of experience. There was a pragmatist in him as well as an existentialist. When he declares, "I make my own circumstance," he is in part merely giving a foolish pep talk, but he is also out-lining a workable strategy for facing the apparent absurdity of circumstances. The world of empty institutions and meaningless slogans, he says, stands as a constant menace. But the individual can turn and face it:

Let him look into its eye and search its nature; inspect its origin . . . ; he will then find in himself a perfect comprehension of its nature and extent; he will have made his hands meet on the other side, and can henceforth defy it and pass on superior. The world is his who can see through its pretension. What deafness, what stone-blind custom, what overgrown error you behold is there only by sufferance,—by your suf-ferenace. See it to be a lie, and you have already dealt it its mortal blow.

This goes a little too far for the twentieth century. When Emerson identifies the "sufferance" of mankind in general with "your sufferance" he crosses the line between stating a fact and claiming for the individual a magical control of the outer world that no one now believes in. In such a mood he can deny the reality of the Fate which on other occasions he affirms with impressive emphasis. But to say that "the world is his who can see through its preten-sion" is not optimistic nonsense if we understand Emerson to mean—as he did mean—that a man can greatly increase the scope of his freedom, can gain and hold ground against Fate and institutions, by being fully aware of the exact circumstances in which he finds himself. Thoreau called this being awake instead of being asleep. What they both tell us is, Take thought. Look the situation over. Don't settle for less than you can get. Honor your doubts and skepticisms. Let the Scholar, says Emerson, "hold by himself; let him add observation to observation, patient of neglect, patient of reproach, and bide his own time . . ." It may well be, as Thoreau says, that most men lead lives of quiet desperation; but it is not invariably necessary that they should. By taking thought we can at least free ourselves from the constraints that are im-posed on us by the force of mere public opinion and the popular cry.

With the help of Emerson and Thoreau I have worked my way back to the familiar ground of Self-Reliance. This is a good stopping-place, but I have the impulse to add one further comment for the benefit of those who share with me the status of pillars of the Establishment. Whereas the young men with knives in their brains are suffering the agonies of choice, we are committed, long ago, by time and habit if by nothing else. Whether we like it or not, we have a stake in society as a going concern; we are the people who keep it going. And by virtue of our experience we know more than these young people do, although maybe not as much as we sometimes think. We readily perceive the comedy of youthful idealism, what Emerson calls "that slight taint of burlesque which in our strange world attaches to the zealot." Yet he reminds us that "these exacting children advertise us of our wants." "By their unconcealed dissatisfaction they expose our poverty and the insignificance of man to man." They pay us the embarrassing [199] compliment of "insatiable expectation." For this reason, "Society also has its duties in reference to this class, and must behold them with what charity it can. Possibly some benefit may yet accrue from them to the state." It is necessary to the comfort of us elders that we should believe in the world and the society we have created and are therefore responsible for. But we know inwardly that our faith is not entirely justified, and these uncommitted young Scholars may in their innocence be able to perceive a truth hidden from us by our perspective of authority. A young woman just out of college said to me recently that Hans Christian Andersen's tale about the Emperor's New Clothes seemed to her a very profound little fable. I have thought about it, and as a citizen of Mr. Henry Luce's new American Empire I am inclined to agree with her.

QUESTIONS FOR DISCUSSION

Understanding the Text

1. Smith states that Emerson's essay is primarily concerned with "how the young American scholar can find a place in American society." What does Emerson say about the scholar's relationship with society? Why is this relationship often hostile? In what respects does the American scholar today feel a similar antagonism or estrangement? Which of the modern American scholar's accusations against society seem to you to be justified? Which are unjustified?

2. The author's discussion of Paul Goodman's *Growing Up Absurd* (1960) suggests that large numbers of young men are "in a worse plight now than ever before" in finding an occupation which challenges their best capacities and in which they can keep their honor and dignity. Discuss this conclusion. Is it still true today? Smith says that Goodman's title "might well stand also as a title for the address on 'The American Scholar.'" Why or why not would Goodman's title be appropriate for Emerson's essay?

3. According to Smith, "The American Scholar" is not "obviously subversive, but its implications amount to a kind of polite anarchy." Discuss the validity of this statement, supporting your view by specific references to Emerson's essay.

4. Smith describes "The American Scholar" as one of Emerson's artistic attempts "to conceive of an ideal character and ideal functions that he could adopt as a guide to his own life." He adds that Emerson's address is "obscure" because his own uncertainties about a vocation did not permit Emerson to "bring into focus the image to which he applies the name of the American Scholar." Do you agree or disagree with this criticism? In what respects is Emerson's picture of the scholar obscure or unclear? What parts of the image seem clear and articulate?

Evaluating Ideas

1. What is your response to the statement that Emerson's viewpoint is "remarkably close to that of the Beat writers of our own day," such as Henry Miller and Jack Kerouac (others would be Allen Ginsberg, Gregory Corso, Lawrence Ferlinghetti, and Gary Snyder)?

2. For illustration of what Emerson calls "cowardly compromise and seeming," Smith draws on William H. Whyte's *The Organization Man* to cite the many college students who accept the corporation ethos, group work, and "the status quo without any inclination to question methods or results." Although Whyte wrote his book in the 1950's, a decade in which college students were reputedly silent and conforming, Smith says students of the 1960's were not much different. He finds the "notion of dangerous radicalism in American universities" to be a "fabrication for political ends" and agrees with Whyte that students are still basically conservative and under the influence of the "organization mentality." Is this still the case in the 1970's, despite today's campus disturbances? Are all the pressures to conform to the organization pattern still operating and being widely accepted by students? Discuss.

3. In what respects can Emerson's scholar be classed as an "Outsider"? Indicate briefly why the following writers and fictional characters belong to the "company of Outsiders": Thoreau, Whitman, Twain, Hemingway; Hester Prynne, Captain Ahab, Huck Finn. What contemporary American writers would you classify as "Outsiders"? Defend your choices. Do you agree with the statement that Emerson's scholar is a literary ancestor of the anti-heroes of contemporary literature? Explain.

4. The essay concludes with Emerson's view that even if the zeal of youthful idealism is sometimes misdirected or even comic, young scholars may intuitively see faults in society which are hidden from an older generation in authority. To what extent is this generalization justified? Can you give examples of this intuitive vision of the young scholar today?

EDUCATION AND SOCIETY

Philip H. Rhinelander

Philip H. Rhinelander is a professor of philosophy and humanities at Stanford University. An administrator and lawyer as well as a teacher, he has a special interest in the philosophy of law and religion.

[2] EMERSON'S PHI Beta Kappa address on the American Scholar—given to the Harvard Chapter in 1837—is probably best known for its strong plea that the American scholar should free himself from blind subservience to European models and European traditions. I am not concerned tonight, however, with this plea for independence, but with a related matter. Near the beginning of his oration, Emerson discussed briefly the problem of individual specialization and the persistent danger, common to all men at all times in all societies, that the living individual might become submerged within his assigned social function. In this situation, Emerson suggested, the concrete man becomes merely a functionary—the player of a role, a *thing* rather than a *man*. This distinction and this danger is a very familiar topic of discussion today by writers of all sorts—writers who see in modern industrial society a special tendency to "depersonalize" the individual and to convert the living, breathing man or woman into a mere functionary separated from his fellows. What is new about this problem today is perhaps the fact that it is not as new as we may be tempted to think. We are faced today, I suggest, with a new and aggravated form of a very ancient and persistent difficulty which has been present, to some extent, in all forms of society. Hence the relevance of what Emerson had to say 130 years ago:

Man is not a farmer, or a professor, or an engineer, but he is all. Man is priest, and scholar, and statesman, and producer, and soldier. In the *divided* or social state

From *The Key Reporter*, XXXIV (Autumn, 1968), 2–4. Reprinted by permission of the author and the United Chapters of Phi Beta Kappa. This address was delivered before the Phi Beta Kappa chapter at Stanford on June 15, 1968.

these functions are parcelled out to individuals, each of whom aims to do his stint of the joint work, whilst each other performs his. . . .

Man is thus metamorphosed into a thing, into many things. The planter, who is Man sent out into the field to gather food, is seldom cheered by any sense of the true dignity of his ministry. He sees his bushel and his cart, and nothing beyond, and sinks into the farmer, instead of Man on the farm. The tradesman scarcely ever gives an ideal worth to his work, but is ridden by the routine of his craft and his soul is subject to dollars. The priest becomes a form; the attorney a statute-book; the mechanic a machine; the sailor a rope of the ship.

In this distribution of functions the scholar is the delegated intellect. In the right state, he is *Man Thinking*. In the degenerate state, when the victim of society, he tends to become a mere thinker, or still worse, the parrot of other men's thinking.

I refer to Emerson not primarily because of what he goes on to say about solving the difficulty, but because of the fact that he *recognized* the difficulty. In the right state of things, the scholar should be *Man Thinking*. But when the scholar is submerged within his specialized function—when he comes merely to be the performer of a separated, social role—then he becomes a *mere thinker* and perhaps no more than a parrot of other men's thinking. Perhaps the difference is a narrow one and hard to formulate with clarity, but it is nevertheless real and deep. On this, I think, Emerson has been proved right. One common threat which runs through all the student unrest which we have seen lately both here and abroad has to do with this very matter. Our colleges and universities have been content to develop mere thinkers; what has been lost (in Emerson's terminology) is the ideal of *Man Thinking*, i.e. the conception of the scholar as first of all a concrete individual engaged in the business of living who is specially qualified by his education to bring to bear the resources of rational thinking upon the solution of the major and pressing problems of human existence and of social justice.

What is the significance of saying that the modern predicament in education is not wholly new but is rather a new and aggravated version of a perennial problem?

First of all, I do not in any way suggest that this is a ground for dismissing the question. I suppose one might take such a position and say that if modern discontent with higher education is concerned chiefly with old problems, there is no need for alarm. I should vehemently reject such a view and argue the reverse. The fact that we are dealing with an ancient problem, presented in new and aggravated forms, is the strongest possible proof that the new disquietude is well grounded and not to be dismissed. We are dealing with a failure of education—failure which has led, in my view, to an increasing doubt in the minds of students (including many of the best students) as to whether intellectual discipline and rational analysis have any relevance to the solution of the pressing problems of the day. I urge those who are going on to careers in scholarship and teaching to make this your primary concern, and to show by teaching and example that this relevance exists.

Secondly, I should urge that if we appreciate the depth of the problem, we may guard ourselves against the temptation to look for superficial solutions. We are all aware that the new convert to a religion or an ideology is apt to be the most violent in his enthusiastic single-mindedness. The same is true of the man who has been newly awakened to a problem; he thinks that because the problem is new to *him*, it must be new to the world, and he tends to dismiss as "apathetic" anybody who does not fully share his new-found sense of frantic urgency. A few years ago, for example, the launching of the first Russian Sputnik precipitated a wild outcry in this country as to the state of scientific education. This had been a matter of great concern for many years previously to many educators who had spoken and written copiously on the subject, without attracting attention. Suddenly, the newly converted rushed in with admonitions and suggestions of all sorts, most of which took no heed of what the experts had been recommending. So here. For years, many thoughtful educators have been concerned about the relative neglect of undergraduate education in America, the ineffectiveness of "liberal education" and the somewhat one-sided emphasis on the development of graduate education and research. Now that their prophecies have been rather alarmingly confirmed, their diagnoses and admonitions have been forgotten and the underlying problems are (in some quarters) being approached as if they were problems of first impression which nobody had previously considered and to which past experience was irrelevant. This may be a natural human reaction, but it is more consonant with Man Thoughtless than with Man Thinking. I would urge that the remedy for bad thinking is good thinking, not the abandonment of thinking,—that the remedy for lack of vision is not blindness but sharper vision.

In this connection, I should like to remind you of some observations of

Alfred North Whitehead in *Science and the Modern World,* from the chapter on "Religion and Science":

In formal logic, a contradiction is the signal of a defeat; but [3] in the evolution of real knowledge it marks the first step in progress toward a victory. This is one great reason for the utmost toleration of variety of opinion. . . . But we have not yet exhausted the discussion of the moral temper required for the pursuit of truth . . . An unflinching determination to take the whole evidence into account is the only method of preservation against the fluctuating extremes of fashionable opinion. This advice seems so easy, and is in fact so difficult to follow.

Let me emphasize two phrases here: First, the *"moral temper* required for the pursuit of truth." Second, the "unflinching determination to take *the whole evidence* into account." The besetting sin of Man Thoughtless (as opposed to Man Thinking) is to over-simplify, to see things in simply black and white, to divide everybody into the "good guys" and the "bad guys," to be intolerant of ambiguity and complexity, to find some single scapegoat on whom to blame all ills, and to reject any evidence which complicates his outlook.

It is fashionable today in some quarters—I use the word "fashionable" as Whitehead did—to blame all our ills indiscriminately upon the structure of society, as if the individual were no more than the helpless victim of social forces. I would suggest to you that if this hypothesis were true, every society would produce conformists and nothing but conformists. The fact is however that every society produces rebels as well as conformists. The social rebel is precisely one who *resists* social pressures to conformity. By his very act of rebellion, therefore, he denies the thesis that society totally controls him. I sympathize with such assertions of independence, but I am puzzled when I hear somebody who seems to be saying (a) the present structure of society compels *all* its members to blind conformity but (b) I, as a member of that society, refuse to conform and demand revolutionary change. The two parts of this assertion seem to destroy each other. If pressures for social conformity could not be resisted, it would be impossible for the individual rebel to exist. On the other hand, if the social rebel exists, then social pressures for conformity cannot be absolute and irresistible.

An illustration of this paradox occurred recently, according to the newspaper accounts of the Phi Beta Kappa exercises at Berkeley. The leading scholar of the graduating class was reported to have said that he had given up everything in his college career to achieve high grades; that he had found the results hollow and empty; and that he deplored the system which had produced this consequence. Such was the news report. Now I wholly sympathize with the first two parts of this statement. To sacrifice everything for grades is to miss most of what college offers, and good grades are no substitute for what is lost. But this has always been true. I could cite a classmate of mine at Harvard who gave everything for grades and, on graduation, likewise regretted his decision. The difference is that my classmate blamed *only himself* for his choice. He did not say, as the young man at Berkeley is reported to have said in effect, "The University is at fault for not protecting me against the choice I made." The last strikes me as counterfeit rebellion, not genuine rebellion. It asserts, not independence, but extreme helplessness. I am not defending the grading system; I wish we might get back to the non-graded system which Stanford followed for its first twenty years. But I have little sympathy for a student who claims that because grades are given, he has no choice but to work solely for grades. Here is a demand, not for freedom, but for stronger paternalism. The objection is not against the individual's being a cog in a machine; it is a demand for a different kind of machine in which he could have been a more contented cog.

This distinction seems to me fundamental. Man Thinking—the true scholar in Emerson's sense—refuses to be a cog in any machine. He insists on being a man rather than a functionary. He takes responsibility for his decisions. And he has confidence that the ability to think rationally—however imperfect such capacities may be—is the best reliance man has in coping with the problems of existence. But the "mere thinker"—the man who considers intellectual pursuits to be no more than a specialized role assigned by society, like being a banker or a sailor or a cafe waiter (in Sartre's celebrated example)— is quite content to be a kind of technician. All he desires, as I have said, is to find a machine in which he can be a contented cog. To those students who find this role profoundly irrelevant in today's world, I can only say that I support you. And I wish you all success in your endeavor to restore Scholarship to a more central and productive place. How this can be done involves many complex questions, as to which I can venture only two brief observations. The first has to do with the structure and organization of colleges and universities, matters much in debate. I would suggest that if one looks at the problem of higher education on a nationwide basis, one must conclude that there is room for a variety of organizations and a variety of structures. I do not believe that there is laid up in some Platonic heaven, the one true model of *the* perfect University. We need in this country colleges and universities of different types to suit different needs. There is a place for the large, public, urban "commuter" university oriented almost entirely toward academic instruction with a minimum of organized student social life, and there is room, at the other end of the spectrum, for the small liberal arts college, perhaps with a religious affiliation and even a requirement for religious discipline. There is, I think, value in variety and flexibility. If this is true, then it is incumbent on any given university, like this one, to choose what sort of institution it wants to be, attracting what sort of students, and performing what kinds of educational functions. We should not let structure determine goals, but begin with the educational goals and adopt whatever kind of administrative structure seems most appropriate to the goals selected.

There is, I repeat, no one form of correct organization, no one correct model of student government, no one correct balance of power as among administration, faculty and students. Many kinds of structure are possible. I make this point because I think some discussions of university affairs have begun at the wrong end by assuming that there is one and only one proper structure for an educational institution to have, and that if that structure were obtained, all else would follow. I believe this view to be mistaken. The educational aims should be controlling—and these unfortunately tend either to be taken for granted without discussion or given only limited discussion.

As to the goals, I should wish to distinguish between knowledge and wisdom. Knowledge, in the sense of learned information, can be transmitted from one man to another and this kind of transmission is part of education, but not the most important part. Wisdom, by contrast, is the capacity to use knowledge effectively for the solution of human problems, is something which cannot be conveyed in the same way, but which each individual must acquire for himself. The process of acquiring wisdom is slow, and none of us has perhaps gotten very far. But here is the point at which the student must, of necessity, be on his own. As has been well said, we can point you the way, but we cannot save you the journey. I make this point because I think that some students today, though they talk of the importance of independent thinking and personal experience, still seem to be looking for a kind of [4] magical infusion and feel cheated when it is not forthcoming. No one can say at this point how much or how little you have gotten from your career at Stanford. If you try to make such estimates I think you will find that you are thinking in terms of knowledge and information, not in terms of that elusive quality, wisdom, which has to do with what will still remain after all you have learned has been forgotten.

I should like to conclude with a particular plea concerning the special difficulty, but also the special importance, of coolness and clear thinking in time of crisis. In his *History of the Peloponnesian War*, Thucydides discussed the social revolution at Corcyra. (Bk. III, ch. 82, 83) in words which seem highly relevant today:

Words changed their ordinary meanings and were construed in new senses. Reckless daring passed for the courage of a loyal partisan, far-sighted hesitation was the excuse of a coward, moderation was the pretext of the unmanly, the power to see all sides of a question was complete inability to act. Impulsive rashness was held the mark of a man, caution in conspiracy was a specious excuse for avoiding action. A violent attitude was always to be trusted, its opponents were suspect. . . . So civil war gave birth to every kind of iniquity in the Greek world. Simplicity, the chief ingredient in a noble nature, was ridiculed and disappeared, and society was divided into rival camps in which no man trusted his fellow. (Trans. Sir Richard Livingstone, Oxford, 1943).

The parallels in today's world scarcely require pointing out. We have new slogans, political and social, used often with calculated ambiguity. Extreme positions, on the right and on the left, are becoming more and more uncompromising. Moderation is taken for apathy, and patience is looked upon as a pretext for inaction. There is mounting unrest and violence not only among university students but in society at large. The product is a weakening of confidence between young and old, between racial groups, between partisan political factions, between students and administrators, between citizens and government. An individualism of suspicion and distrust is replacing an individualism of opportunity and hope.

The key word in the passage from Thucydides is *euethes*, which Sir Richard Livingstone translates "simplicity." It is called "the chief ingredient in a noble nature." Like the English word "simplicity," the Greek word *euethes* may be used in a commendatory or derogatory sense. It may mean good-hearted, kind and without guile, or it may mean gullible. The double sense is, I think, significant. The word denotes the characteristic of man which gives and evokes trust. Because simplicity is trusting, it can be deceived and victimized, but this very weakness is its strength. By trusting others it invites reciprocal trust, thereby laying the foundation for communication and mutual cooperation.

It is this quality, I believe, that Man Thinking—the true scholar—must try above all else to maintain and to defend. Education ought to be ultimately not a matter of systems, nor of organizations, or of structures, or of theories, but of individuals who *encounter* one another, who respect one another, who can speak to one another, despite disagreement, and who can *listen*.

QUESTIONS FOR DISCUSSION

Understanding the Text

1. This essay focuses on Emerson's idea that the individual may be so submerged in his assigned social function that he "becomes merely a functionary—the player of a role, a *thing* rather than a *man*." Rhinelander says that today we are faced with a "new and aggravated form" of this difficulty. What are some of his reasons for holding this opinion? What additional evidence of our predicament can you supply? Can the college student himself be regarded as a mere functionary or role player? Explain.

2. In his discussion of the two college students who "gave everything for grades," Rhinelander distinguishes between counterfeit rebellion and genuine rebellion. What is the distinction? Can you illustrate it further from your own experience? Give details.

3. How does the author contrast Emerson's Man Thinking and the "mere thinker"? Can you illustrate the contrast in different terms. If so, what are they?

4. How are knowledge and wisdom differentiated in the essay? What is their relative importance in your education? What does Emerson say in "The American Scholar" about "the importance of independent thinking and personal experience" in the acquisition of wisdom?

Evaluating Ideas

1. Rhinelander suggests that the failure of education has led to "an increasing doubt in the minds of students (including many of the best students) as to whether intellectual discipline and rational analysis have any relevance to the solution of the pressing problems of the day." Do you agree or disagree that this is the case? Support your answer.

2. After arguing for variety and flexibility in American colleges and universities, Rhinelander says that specific educational goals should determine an institution's administrative structure. He applies the same argument to forms of student government. What are the educational aims of student government in your own college or

university? In what respects is the administrative structure of student government appropriate or inappropriate to carry out these aims?

3. The author supports the view that "the chief ingredient in a noble nature" is what Thucydides called *euethes*, "simplicity"—"the characteristic of man which gives and evokes trust." Do you agree that this is the quality that the American scholar, or Man Thinking, "must try above all else to maintain and to defend"? What other qualities seem to you to be of critical importance in the American scholar today?

TOPICS FOR THEMES

Many of the Questions for Discussion after each essay provide suitable subjects for written as well as oral discussion. Following are additional topics for themes.

1. Is Emerson's view of the scholar possible of fulfillment today, or is it useful primarily as an ideal? Consider in detail the practicability of Emerson's essay.

2. In defining the scholar as Man Thinking, Emerson elaborates his definition in considerable detail. Many other views of the scholar are possible. Write a theme of definition in which you give your own detailed conception of the scholar.

3. Most critics see Emerson's scholar as an Outsider in conflict with the values of nineteenth-century American society. Write a theme on the scholar today as an Outsider, identifying the contemporary social values which he should resist. Or consider the scholar in the opposite way, as a defender of our cultural heritage. Write a theme on the scholar as an Insider, noting the contemporary social values which he should defend.

4. Compare or contrast the scholar (either student or teacher) as you find him in your college, with the scholar as you think he ought to be.

5. Analyze the advantages of the modern college environment in furthering the development of the scholar. Or consider the practical obstacles in that environment which hinder the growth of the scholar. Or combine your analyses of the positive and negative environmental factors in a single essay.

6. Write a theme comparing the treatment of Emerson's address by Perry, Erskine, Smith, and Rhinelander. Observe especially how the four writers agree or disagree on the meaning and value of Emerson's essay.

7. Write a long essay or term paper entitled "The American Scholar Today." Your instructor may give specific directions about the length, content, and structure of your paper. For example, he may want you to follow Emerson's structural pattern (definition of the scholar, influences on the scholar, duties of the scholar, etc.), or he may want you to work out your own structure.

8. In "Education and Society," Rhinelander selects a single major idea in Emerson's essay—the distinction between Man Thinking and the "mere thinker" or functionary—and develops it by detailed application and illustration. Choose a different idea from "The American Scholar" and develop it in an essay.

9. Consider carefully the following excerpt from Emerson's *Essays* (1841): "But do your thing, and I shall know you. Do your work and you shall reinforce yourself. A man must consider what a blind-man's-buff is this game of conformity." Discuss the relationship of the passage to "The American Scholar."

BIBLIOGRAPHICAL SUGGESTIONS

The student who wishes to read additional commentaries on Emerson's "The American Scholar" will find the following essays informative: Guy Stanton Fo.d, "The American Scholar To-day," *School and Society*, XL (November 17, 1934), 641–651; Leo Marx, "The American Scholar Today," *Commentary*, XXXII (July, 1961), 48–53; David Mead, "Emerson's Scholar and the Scholars," *Journal of Higher Education*, XL (November, 1969), 649–660; William Allan Neilson, "The American Scholar Today," *The American Scholar*, V (Spring, 1936), 149–163; Henry Nash Smith, "Emerson's Problem of Vocation: A Note on 'The American Scholar,'" *The New England Quarterly*, XII (March, 1939), 52–67; Charles F. Thwing, "The American Scholar: Emerson's Phi Beta Kappa Address (1837)," *The Hibbert Journal*, XXXVI (October, 1937), 119–131; Harvey Wish, "Emerson's Scholar Reconsidered," *The Journal of Higher Education*, XXXV (December, 1964), 475–480.

The standard edition of Emerson's works is Edward Waldo Emerson, ed., *The Complete Works of Ralph Waldo Emerson* (Boston and New York: Houghton Mifflin Company, 1903–4), 12 volumes. The most complete collection of Emerson's correspondence is Ralph L. Rusk, ed., *The Letters of Ralph Waldo Emerson* (New York: Columbia University Press, 1939), 6 volumes.

A definitive edition of Emerson's works is in the process of being published by the Harvard University Press. The new edition includes Stephen E. Whicher, Robert E. Spiller, and Wallace E. Williams, eds., *The Early Lectures of Ralph Waldo Emerson* (Cambridge, Massachusetts: Harvard University Press, 1959–   ). Several volumes of the new edition of Emerson's journals and notebooks have been published: William H. Gilman, Alfred R. Ferguson, Merrell R. Davis, Merton M. Sealts, Jr., Harrison Hayford, and George P. Clark, eds., *The Journals and Miscellaneous Notebooks of Ralph Waldo Emerson* (Cambridge, Massachusetts: Harvard University Press, 1960–   ). Until the new edition of Emerson's journals is completed, it can be supplemented with the older standard edition: Edward Waldo Emerson and Waldo Emerson Forbes, eds., *The Journals of Ralph Waldo Emerson* (Boston and New York: Houghton Mifflin Company, 1909–14), 10 volumes.

A useful general introduction to Emerson and his writing is Frederic I. Carpenter, *Emerson Handbook* (New York: Hendricks House, Inc., 1953). The most comprehensive biography is Ralph L. Rusk, *The Life of Ralph Waldo Emerson* (New York: Charles Scribner's Sons, 1949). For the student who wishes to study Emerson's thought and artistry more extensively, two books are especially informative: Sherman Paul, *Emerson's Angle of Vision* (Cambridge, Massachusetts: Harvard University Press, 1952); and Stephen E. Whicher, *Freedom and Fate: An Inner Life of Ralph Waldo Emerson* (Philadelphia: University of Pennsylvania Press, 1953).

DATE DUE

NOV 2 8 '88			